Praise for *How to Grow*

God wants us to grow. But without a plan, growth will remain an aspiration instead of a reality. *How to Grow* provides a robust, practical, and habit-based plan to help individuals and churches become more intentional in pursuing transformation. If you're interested in growing and helping others grow, then you'll appreciate this book.

ED STETZER
Billy Graham Chair of Church, Mission, and Evangelism at Wheaton College, and Executive Director of the Billy Graham Center

I've become such an admirer of Darryl Dash in the several years I've known him, and I'm grateful to see his pastoral and practical wisdom poured into these pages. Without a doubt, people will read *How to Grow* and discover habits to help them grow in Christ. This will now be the first book I turn to in my own discipleship relationships.

JEN POLLOCK MICHEL
Author of *Teach Us to Want* and *Keeping Place*

Deeply simple. Profoundly accessible. Generously gracious. Here are three phrases that describe *How to Grow*. In his book, Darryl outlines a refreshing approach to an ancient practice—spiritual growth. So don't miss this, and don't read it too fast either—take it one step at a time.

DANIEL IM
Author of *No Silver Bullets*, coauthor of *Planting Missional Churches*, director of church multiplication at NewChurches.com, podcaster, and teaching pastor

Discipleship is a key but often neglected part of Christian life and ministry. Without intentionality, it simply won't happen. I'm encouraged to see Darryl exploring this important topic, and pray that this book will be a blessing to the church.

TIM CHALLIES
Author of *Do More Better*, and blogger at challies.com

While we may say we believe the gospel, most of us aren't changed by it. *How to Grow* is about how to get the gospel in you—not through more information but through desire-forming habits. Darryl Dash's book is a hopeful and practical pathway for personal and communal transformation: one that combats "try harder and know more" with the explosive power of grace.

ASHLEY HALES
Pastor's wife, and author of *Finding Holy in the Suburbs*

If you're frustrated by the long lists of do's and don'ts often found in books on spiritual growth, you'll find *How to Grow* refreshingly straightforward and relevant. Filled with relatable stories, reflection questions, and actionable next steps, this book invites readers to grow into the full life found in Jesus Christ, not just in the eternity to come but in our daily lives right where we are.

ASHERITAH CIUCIU
Founder of One Thing Alone Ministries, and author of *Full: Food, Jesus, and the Battle for Satisfaction* and *He Is Enough: Living in the Fullness of Jesus*

Darryl Dash has an ability to present the truth in memorable and inviting ways. This book will be another good contribution to the community of faith.

TREVIN WAX
Author of *This Is Our Time*, Bible and Reference Publisher at LifeWay Christian Resources, and managing editor of The Gospel Project

I cannot overstate my enthusiasm for Darryl Dash's project *How to Grow*. Though there are plenty of books on the classic spiritual disciplines, there are precious few that equip believers for practicing spiritual disciplines as a means of grace—as habits of the heart integrated into the whole of life. I will rejoice when this book gets published.

SCOTTY WARD SMITH
Teacher in Residence at West End Community Church, Nashville, TN, professor, and author of *Everyday Prayers*

Luther once said that to progress is always to begin again. In other words, Christian growth is not so much about reaching one new level of spirituality after the next as it is about returning, again and again, to the same grace that saved us in the first place. 'Tis grace that brought us safe thus far, and grace will lead us home. Few resources help us in this grace journey as clearly and effectively as *How to Grow* does. I look forward not only to benefitting from Darryl's guidance myself, but also to sharing it with friends and congregants who long for progress in their journey toward becoming like Christ.

SCOTT SAULS
Pastor of Christ Presbyterian Church, and author of *From Weakness to Strength* and *Irresistible Faith*

The thing I love most about *How to Grow* is that Dash approaches spiritual discipleship holistically. He understands that there's no sacred/secular divide, and all of life can be worship and an opportunity to grow closer to Christ. Dash teaches people how to truly be successful in applying the gospel to all areas of life, because he understands that it's only by God's grace.

CHELSEA PATTERSON SOBOLIK
Author of *Longing for Motherhood*

I like this book a lot. It is simple, clear, biblically faithful, and extremely practical. Written by a pastor with experience in the stop and start nature of spiritual growth.

MEZ MCCONNELL
Founder of 20schemes, and author of *Church in Hard Places*

APPLYING
THE GOSPEL
TO ALL OF YOUR LIFE

HOW TO

GROW

DARRYL DASH

MOODY PUBLISHERS

CHICAGO

Unless otherwise noted, all Scripture quotations are taken from the ESV® Bible (The Holy Bible, English Standard Version®), copyright © 2001 by Crossway, a publishing ministry of Good News Publishers. Used by permission. All rights reserved.

Scripture quotations marked CSB are taken from the Christian Standard Bible®, Copyright © 2017 by Holman Bible Publishers. Used by permission. Christian Standard Bible®, and CSB® are federally registered trademarks of Holman Bible Publishers.

Emphasis in Scripture has been added.

Published in association with the literary agency of **The Steve Laube Agency, 24 W. Camelback Rd. A635, Phoenix, AZ 85013**

Edited by Connor Sterchi
Cover and interior design: Erik M. Peterson
Cover illustration of plants copyright (c) 2017 by IkonStudio/iStock (807446304). All rights reserved.
Author photo: Froz'n Motion Photography

Library of Congress Cataloging-in-Publication Data

Names: Dash, Darryl, author.
Title: How to grow : applying the gospel to all of your life / by Darryl Dash.
Description: Chicago : Moody Publishers, [2018] | Includes bibliographical
  references.
Identifiers: LCCN 2018014095 (print) | LCCN 2018020688 (ebook) | ISBN
  9780802496683 (ebook) | ISBN 9780802418197
Subjects: LCSH: Spiritual formation.
Classification: LCC BV4511 (ebook) | LCC BV4511 .D37 2018 (print) | DDC
  248.4--dc23
LC record available at https://lccn.loc.gov/2018014095

ISBN-13: 978-0-8024-1819-7

We hope you enjoy this book from Moody Publishers. Our goal is to provide high-quality, thought-provoking books and products that connect truth to your real needs and challenges. For more information on other books and products written and produced from a biblical perspective, go to www.moodypublishers.com or write to:

Moody Publishers
820 N. LaSalle Boulevard
Chicago, IL 60610

1 3 5 7 9 10 8 6 4 2

For Charlene,
who not only helped to shape this book,
but embodies its message.

CONTENTS

FOREWORD

I grew up in the church, but it was a long time before I grew in the church.

Oh, sure, I got older just like everybody else; there's no defeating time. But it wasn't until I was older that I started to grow, at least in any consistent manner and with any cooperation from myself. The Holy Spirit is faithful, of course, and He was doing a billion things in my life every year since my conversion, but it wasn't until I wakened one fateful, broken day to the beauty of *how* I was growing that my growth really "took off."

Maybe I'd read 2 Corinthians 3:18 before that day, but I don't remember having done so:

> And we all, with unveiled face, beholding the glory of
> the Lord, are being transformed into the same image
> from one degree of glory to another. For this comes
> from the Lord who is the Spirit.

I probably could have told you that real transformation comes by the Spirit, but I probably wouldn't have told you that it had much to do with looking at Jesus. No, real spiritual growth comes from finally getting your act together.

Or so I thought.

The only problem was that I was terrible at getting my act together. Maybe you are too. If so, you've come to the right book.

There are lots of practical helps in this book—the Christian life is imminently applicable—but you won't find self-help, moralistic, therapeutic spirituality here. Nor will you find nose-to-the-grindstone law-abiding as the silver bullet to your discipleship problems.

There's something about beholding the glory of Jesus. It doesn't make us not work. But it makes us work in a new way.

The apostle Paul puts it this way elsewhere in Titus 2:11–12:

> For the grace of God has appeared, bringing salvation
> for all people, training us to renounce ungodliness
> and worldly passions, and to live self-controlled,
> upright, and godly lives in the present age.

Darryl Dash knows we need to train. He knows no growth comes without the disciplines of following Jesus. That's why there are chapters on steps and habits. But Darryl also knows that training is a nonstarter without the "appearance"—*epiphaneia* (an epiphany!)—of grace getting it all moving.

That's what happened to me that day I finally started to figure out how to grow. I had an epiphany of grace. And all the visions of perfectly upward discipleship trajectories fell away in the blazing glory of the Christ who is my righteousness.

Man, I'm glad you have this book in your hands! You will find in the pages that follow a reliable guide to Christian practice, a pastoral mentor for as long as you're reading toward confidence in following Jesus, and above all of that, a consistent pointer to the finished work of Christ as the motivation, empowerment, and validation of your pursuit of knowledge, worship, and obedience.

I am grateful for the all the churches I grew up in. But I'm more thankful still for the day I started to grow. I hope this book will serve the same purpose for you. Because He who promised is faithful, and He will complete the good work He began in you. Now, thanks to *How to Grow*, you've got a faithful companion for responding to the Spirit's work in your life.

I pray you will turn the last page changed and renewed. Go ahead and start. You've got nothing to lose.

Jared C. Wilson
Midwestern Baptist Theological Seminary
Kansas City, Missouri

INTRODUCTION

I've been a pastor for over twenty-five years. For most of that time, I've pastored established churches with existing ministries. I stepped into the existing structures and fulfilled my expected role. I preached, taught, led, and cared for people. I began to notice that it was easy to go through the motions in ministry. Some people changed, while others seemed stuck. I grew increasingly frustrated, and sensed that something was missing.

Then, a few years ago my wife and I had the privilege of planting a new church in downtown Toronto. I realized we had the opportunity to design a ministry structure from scratch. We did that, but I still sensed I was largely repeating my past ministry experience. It was too easy, even in a new church, to go through the motions and expect people to grow simply by showing up.

I began to dig deeper into what it takes to grow spiritually, and to facilitate spiritual growth in others. I began to view discipleship differently, exploring the roles desire and joy play in our spiritual lives as well as the importance of our habits. I also found inspiration from an unlikely source: a nutrition company that does a better job discipling people into their worldview than any church I had pastored. My wife and I began to dream about discipling the people in our church just as effectively. I began to learn everything I could about their methods and to reflect on the theological and practical aspects of how we grow in our faith.

Churches have been discipling people for centuries, and it would be arrogant and foolish to pretend that I've reinvented discipleship or discovered the missing key to spiritual growth. But I have developed a usable, habit-based approach that is also theologically rich, strategic, and practical. This book is a guide to change, and I hope it will unleash a passionate desire for spiritual growth in your own life.

Rather than providing you with a complete theology of spiritual growth or sanctification, my goal is to explore the riches of Scriptural truth so that we see and experience spiritual growth differently. I crave truth that reverberates in the soul, rewires our thinking, and compels us to live differently. The first few chapters of the book unpack what we need to know about the gospel so that we have a strong foundation upon which we can build our practices.

Because I'm writing for people like me who want to know what steps to take to grow in every part of their lives, I also want to give you practical tools you can use right now. Each chapter ends with application questions. I encourage you to pause and reflect on those questions so you get maximum benefit from this book. As the book unfolds, I'm going to describe some practical steps you can take to begin creating change in your life. You can take these steps whether you're a skeptic, someone who's curious about Christianity, a mature believer, or anywhere in between. These steps will set you up for a lifetime of spiritual growth so that you become who you were meant to be.

When we think of a mature disciple of Christ, most of us think of a certain kind of person. They are more put together than we are—at least it looks that way. Most of us don't feel like we have it all together. We face overwhelming priorities, car repairs, screaming children, job stress, money worries, and more. Who's got time to focus on spiritual growth?

But the truth is we need to know how to grow in the midst of our chaotic, messy lives. And the good news is that Jesus embraces the battered, bruised, and imperfect. His grace meets us in our need and changes us in ways we could never imagine. I believe you can experience the change you're looking for, and that you can also influence the lives of more people than you realize.

Here's what you can expect. We're going to begin by looking at the best news ever, and how it's the key to transformation. We'll examine why growth is important, and also how it's different from what we usually think. I'll give you practical tools to identify your current stage, take the next step, and build practices that will help you grow. And I'll show you how you can make a difference in the lives of others.

Let's get started.

CHAPTER ONE

THE BEST NEWS EVER AND WHAT IT MEANS FOR YOU

We never "get beyond the gospel" to something more advanced.
The gospel is not the first step in a stairway of truths;
rather, it is more like the hub in a wheel of truth.
The gospel is not just the ABCs but the A to Z of Christianity.

TIMOTHY KELLER, *THE CENTRALITY OF THE GOSPEL*

The one thing the gospel never does is nothing.

RAY ORTLUND JR., *THE GOSPEL*

Lola was a slave.

She grew up in a poor family in a rural part of the Philippines. She was penniless, unschooled, and gullible. Her parents wanted her to marry a pig farmer twice her age, but she was unhappy at the prospect. When a lieutenant approached her with an offer, she couldn't resist: she could have food and shelter if she would commit to taking care of his young daughter.

Lola agreed. She had no idea she had signed up to become a slave for life.

Lola lived with that daughter, and eventually her children and grandchildren, for fifty-six years, both in the Philippines and America. She raised children. She cooked and cleaned from dawn to dark. She was tongue-lashed and beaten, wore used clothing, and ate scraps and leftovers by herself in the kitchen. She slept anywhere she could find a spot: on couches, in storage areas, in corners, or on piles of laundry.

As Alex, the son of the family that enslaved Lola, grew up he began to understand that Lola was a slave. As a young adult, he gave her an ATM card linked to his account and taught her how to use it. He tried to teach her how to drive.

Later he invited Lola to live with him and his family. He gave her a bedroom and permission to do whatever she wanted: sleep in, watch TV, or do nothing all day. "She could relax—and be free—for the first time in her life. I should have known it wouldn't be that simple," he writes in a recent article for *The Atlantic*. He sat her down. "This is your house now . . . you're not here to serve us. You can relax, okay?"

"Okay," she said. And went back to cleaning. She didn't know how *not* to be a slave.

One day he came home and found Lola sitting on the couch with her feet up, doing a word puzzle and watching TV, with a cup of tea beside her. She looked up sheepishly. "Progress," he thought.[1]

Lola had been a slave for so long that she struggled to embrace freedom when it was offered her. She spent the last years of her life with only a fleeting understanding that she was free and loved.

In a similar way, many of us find it difficult to accept our freedom in Christ. The Bible says that we—all of us—have lived as slaves to sin (John 8:34; Rom. 6:20). We're so used to it that we struggle to understand that, in Jesus, we're no longer slaves. We'll spend the rest of our lives trying to live in light of two truths we find hard to grasp: in Jesus we're free and we're loved.

WHAT IS THE GOSPEL?

A Christian leader once argued that we should take the next ten years off so that we could define the gospel.

He was right and he was wrong. We do need to define the gospel. There's nothing more important than understanding, at the deepest levels of our souls, the truth of what God has done for us in Jesus. The gospel is both simple and complex. A small child can understand it—sometimes better than we can—but the most advanced theologian will never be able to sound its deepest depths.

Yet we can't wait ten years to define the gospel. We need the gospel *now*. We can no sooner take ten years to define the gospel than we could take a ten-year break from breathing. The gospel is the desperate need of the world and of every human heart. It's of first importance. Our churches need it. We need it if we have any hope of becoming who we were meant to be, because the gospel is the key to spiritual growth.

> *The gospel is the key to spiritual growth.*

So what is the gospel? The gospel is set within a larger story of a good world that's gone bad because of human sin. Unless we understand the larger story, it's impossible to understand the gospel itself. The Bible tells one unified story that explains our world, and the centerpiece of that story is the gospel.

God created all things good, including us, but we rebelled against Him. We see evidence of the brokenness of the world all around us: wars, violence, injustice, inequity, relational breakdown, natural disasters, sickness, death, and more. The world is broken beyond our ability to fix it. Not only is the world broken, but so are we. But God didn't create the world like this. We've contaminated the world through our treason against a good and holy God.

We made such a mess of this world that God would have been justified in writing us off. He would be right to judge us and be done with us. But instead, God chose to rescue us. God—one God who is three persons: Father, Son, and Holy Spirit—conspired together to save us. The Father sent His Son, Jesus, to become one of us. Instead of destroying the world, He entered it. When Jesus was born, He became the first person in history to live without rebelling against God. His obedience was perfect. Jesus also gave us a taste of life the way it should be. He healed the sick, served outcasts, and confronted injustice. The miracles He performed foreshadowed the day when God will restore the world to the way it should be.

But that's not even the best part. Although Jesus was the first truly innocent person to ever live, He took our place and died as payment for sins we committed. He repeatedly emphasized that this is why He came. He not only entered the world filled with people who deserved to be judged, but He took that judgment on Himself so we don't have to. And by doing this, He restored us to relationship with our heavenly Father.

To everyone's surprise, Jesus' followers found His grave empty three days after He'd been killed. Over five hundred people saw Him alive before He ascended to heaven. His resurrection proved that what He said was true. It vindicated Him. It also shows us that we can trust Him, and it gives a preview of what will happen to those who follow Him.

One day Jesus will return and judge all of us, and then He'll completely renew our world. Those who have trusted Jesus will enjoy the world as it was meant to be, in perfect relationship with God and others.

But now, God calls for our response. God invites us to come to Him in surrender, admitting our need. God calls us to admit the truth about ourselves, to turn away from our sins, and follow Him in faith and trust. There's only one way out of the mess we find ourselves in, and that's through Jesus. We've been found guilty, but Jesus has already paid the penalty for those who put their trust in Him. If we cling to our own efforts to pay that penalty, we'll miss out on what Jesus has done and face the penalty ourselves—a penalty that's more than we can ever pay. We *must* take advantage of the gospel. It's our only hope.

Until Jesus comes back, the church's role is to show and tell the story of the gospel. The gospel motivates us, guides us, and empowers us. It calls for a response. Once we respond with genuine repentance and faith, the gospel changes everything.

Whew. That's a lot, yet it's barely scratching the surface of what the gospel means. To simplify it a bit more, the gospel can be summarized by understanding three truths:

- **God is holy.**
- **Humanity is sinful.**
- **God is rescuing His people and creation through the perfect work of Jesus Christ.**

These truths set everything right. They not only show us the way to be right with God, but they also show us the way to live. The best news of all is that God's rescue is completely based on grace. We don't earn any of it. We don't deserve it. But it's ours, given to us freely by God.

That's the best news ever. Paul, a former enemy of Jesus who became one of His most passionate followers, wrote that we stand in this gospel, and that we're being saved by it. "For I delivered to you as of first importance what I also received: that Christ died for our sins in accordance with the Scriptures, that he was buried, that he was raised on the third day in accordance with the Scriptures" (1 Cor. 15:3–4). It's the very power of God, and the greatest truth known by humanity, yet we often treat it like it doesn't matter. The apostle Paul observed this tendency even in the first century, writing to the Galatian believers: "I am astonished that you are so quickly deserting him who called you in the grace of Christ and are turning to a different gospel—not that there is another one" (Gal. 1:6–7). This has been our story ever since.

It's time to rediscover the good news that has the power to change our lives forever.

WHAT THIS MEANS FOR YOU

Because the work of Jesus is the climactic event of history and the transformative truth in our lives, we can look to it in every aspect of our lives. In fact, most of the New Testament is spent unpacking how it applies to every part of life. Simply open to any New Testament passage to discover an aspect of the gospel being applied to real life.

While there's no way I can tease out all the implications of this amazing news, I'd like to highlight a few things that are true in your life if you have trusted Jesus.

1. *You're Free from Guilt and Shame*

Most of us are familiar with *shame*: the internal sense that we don't measure up and that we're not okay. It's an emotional weapon Satan uses to corrupt our relationships with God and each other, and to disintegrate our vocational vision and creativity.[2] Brené Brown's TED talk on the subject has been viewed over 34 million times,[3] and her books on vulnerability and imperfection are bestsellers.

We also experience *guilt*: the objective sense that we haven't met an external standard. Although widespread acceptance of religion seems to be declining, we still seem to struggle with guilt. According to professor Wilfred M. McClay, "Guilt has not merely lingered. It has grown, even metastasized, into an ever more powerful and pervasive element in the life of the contemporary West."[4] Yet we still don't know what to do with it.

The gospel provides the remedy we need. For those who trust Jesus, every wrong done and every good left undone—past, present, and future—has been dealt with at the cross. Jesus has made full payment, so that when God looks at us He sees the perfect righteousness of Jesus. The Bible offers this shocking declaration: "There is therefore now no condemnation for those who are in Christ Jesus" (Rom. 8:1). We are free from sin, guilt, and shame.

One of my favorite stories in the Bible is found in Zechariah 3. Zechariah has a vision of Joshua, the high priest, standing in God's presence. It was the Day of Atonement, which means that Joshua would have spent days preparing himself so that he could be pure before God. In Zechariah's vision, though, Joshua stood before God with dirty clothes. The language that Zechariah uses is explicit: he was covered in excrement. To make it worse, Satan was also present and accusing Joshua of his failings.

That's a pretty good picture of how the best of us measure up before God. My friend Brian Bakke regularly sweeps the streets where he lives to remind himself of how we measure up before God. He writes:

> I clean the block each morning. And as I gather up the
> drug bags, dog crap, food garbage, butts, and bottles,
> I think this is how I look before a pure and holy God
> on my best day. I am covered in my own filth as I
> stand before the Almighty. And as I put my hands in
> filth I am reminded [that] God left Heaven and came

to live in our filth. And He redeemed it. In this way He calls me to be an act of redemption on my street and redeem the places where people dump trash. Where they seek to kill themselves or others. And to get in the way. The entire time I am asking God to forgive our fathers for the sins that created this neighborhood and city, and then ask God to bless the saints who live here, that we can be salt and light. And take back from Satan the land he stole from Jesus.[5]

We need the gospel. We're hopeless before God without it. In Zechariah's vision, God told Satan to shut up. He took away Joshua's filthy clothes and reclothed him like royalty. This demonstrates what God does for each one of us when we come to Him.

When we feel guilt, shame, or regret, we can remember that God has silenced our accuser, removed our guilt, and reclothed us with His righteousness. He has decisively dealt with our sins—not just some of them, but all of them. Martin Luther, a priest who struggled with guilt more than five hundred years ago, discovered the gospel's power in dealing with sin and offers advice that still holds true today:

> When the devil throws our sins up to us and declares that we deserve death and hell, we ought to speak thus: "I admit that I deserve death and hell. What of it? Does this mean that I shall be sentenced to eternal damnation? By no means. For I know One who suffered and made satisfaction in my behalf. His name is Jesus Christ, the Son of God. Where he is, there I shall be also."[6]

The gospel removes all condemnation from your life. We'll still encounter guilt and shame as long as we live, but we can keep turning to the gospel to remind ourselves that in Jesus we're forgiven and reclothed in honor. Whenever we feel that we don't measure up, we can remind ourselves that God removes our shame. Because Jesus measures up, all who trust Jesus measure up too.

2. You're Loved and Accepted

Shea Glover, an eighteen-year-old high school student from Chicago, recently conducted a social experiment at her school. She recorded video of classmates, capturing their reactions before and after she explained her purpose: "I'm taking pictures of things I find beautiful." After being called beautiful, almost every face lit up with joy.[7] We can't help but light up when we're appreciated.

We tend to think that God tolerates us but can't possibly be very happy with us. The gospel corrects us by announcing that, although we did nothing to deserve it, we are intimately loved and accepted by God. The prophet Zephaniah, at the end of an Old Testament book that includes some stern warnings for the people of God, wrote this startling truth:

> "The Lord your God is in your midst,
>   a mighty one who will save;
> he will rejoice over you with gladness;
>   he will quiet you by his love;
> he will exult over you with loud singing."
>   (Zeph. 3:17)

Isn't that staggering? God doesn't just tolerate us; He rejoices over us. He exults over us with loud singing. To *exult* means to express great joy, and can even include actions like leaping, shrieking ecstatically, and shouting with joy. God isn't reserved in His affections for His people. He overflows in love for us. We can now approach God like a young son approaches his loving father (Rom. 8:15). And hard things somehow seem easier when we know we're loved.

Jesus Himself said, "Greater love has no one than this, that someone lay down his life for his friends" (John 15:13). Jesus' work is both the foundation of and the greatest evidence of God's love for us. On the basis of this good news, nothing can separate us from God's love (Rom. 8:35). We can't mess it up. God doesn't just tolerate us. He lavishes us with love. We apply the gospel when we remind ourselves of His love, and enter into the relationship Jesus has made possible for us. Because of the gospel, we enjoy intimacy with God Himself.

Remind yourself regularly: God loves those who trust Him. You are loved. Keep yourself close to this love (Jude 1:21).

3. You've Been Given the Power to Change

I once tried to ride a bike forty miles uphill. That may seem like nothing, but it was more than I could handle. I had to call my wife Charlene to come pick me up and drive me and the bike the rest of the way.

> *He rewires us so that we don't just* act *differently, but we* desire *differently. We begin to love the things that he loves.*

In the same way, we lack the power to change ourselves. The story of the Bible is the story of human inability to obey God—at least until Jesus came. Jesus' birth changed everything. When we believe, God gives us new hearts so that we want to obey Him (Ezek. 36:26). He rewires us so that we don't just *act* differently, but we *desire* differently. We begin to love the things that He loves. He gives us new desires (Ps. 37:4).

And God gives us the Holy Spirit to empower our obedience. When we follow Jesus, the same power that raised Jesus from the dead begins to work in us (Eph. 1:19–20). He begins to develop new characteristics within us: love, joy, peace, patience, kindness, goodness, faithfulness, gentleness, and self-control (Gal. 5:22–23). God guarantees that He will finish the work in us that He's started (Phil. 1:6). He always finishes what He starts.

Of course we play a role. In his letter to the Philippians, Paul encouraged his readers to work out their salvation with fear and trembling. But even this is a product of God's work within us. In the very next verse, Paul says it's *God* who works in us so that we desire and act in new ways (Phil. 2:12–13). In fact, our role involves discipline and hard work (1 Cor. 9:27). But even our role is powered by God. Our hard work is necessary, but it's only possible because God is empowering us to do this work.

An older friend told me that he biked through Holland. I was impressed by his athleticism until he told me that he used an e-bike. I don't mean to insult e-bike riders, but I'm not sure you can say *you* cycled through Holland if your bike has an electric motor.

Once we follow Jesus, we're all spiritual e-bikers. Nobody operates on their own power. God starts to work on us and gives us a power that we never had before. He's renovating us from the inside out. When we struggle to change, we can remind ourselves that God has given us new hearts, and that He's also given us the Holy Spirit to change and empower us. He gives us the power to change, and He always finishes what He's started.

4. You're Part of a New Family

Churches often don't look like much. I'm not talking about the buildings; I'm talking about the people. It seems that they're full of people like us: people who are imperfect, inconvenient, sometimes disappointing, and always a lot of work. But they're also beautiful. Churches display the glory and wisdom of God. At their best they are foretastes of heaven. They're where we grow, where we love and are loved, and where we learn what it means to be part of God's family.

One of the greatest gifts God gives us through the gospel is membership in His family so that we don't have to live alone.

When I was a child, my father lived in Margate, a small resort town in southeast England. I lived in Canada and didn't see him regularly. My mother put my sister and me on a plane to visit him when I was twelve, which was one of the hardest things she'd ever done. She wanted us to know our dad, but she also knew that because of the complexity of international custody laws, she might never see us again.

I remember feeling lonely when we landed since I knew only one person on the continent, and I wasn't sure I could rely on him. But Dad picked us up promptly, which was a little reassuring. I still felt unsure of what would happen, though.

On our first Sunday we found our way to the Baptist church off the town square. I didn't know anyone there. I remember taking the bread and juice during Communion at the end of the service, and somehow felt like I was no longer alone. I can't explain it. I just felt like I was with family. I somehow knew that I could count on these people if needed because the gospel had made me family with them. I knew, even at that age, that God's people are everywhere on earth.

Churches display the glory and wisdom of God. At their best they are foretastes of heaven. They're where we grow, where we love and are loved, and where we learn what it means to be part of God's family.

I felt this way again in Madison, Wisconsin, last year. Charlene and I ate at a restaurant in the town square. I knew only one person in the area and felt far from home. When food arrived at a nearby table, I watched as strangers bowed to thank God.

I didn't know them, but I experienced the same feeling of belonging. I knew we belonged together. Those of us who are in Christ have a big family. We're never alone.

What's true globally is also true locally. Because we started a church from scratch, I didn't have many people in my church family a few years ago. I'm glad I do now. As the church grew, so did my family. My local church family has faces and names. We laugh together, pray together, and learn from one another. It's not perfect; we annoy each other too, but that's okay. I love knowing that I'm not alone, and that I have people who are watching out for me, just as I'm watching out for them. We have nothing in common except for Jesus, and that's enough. Family isn't merely a metaphor: we are brothers and sisters because of the gospel.

This means that it's important to take our spiritual family seriously. When we understand that the local church is a family of brothers and sisters, we'll make it a priority in our lives. We won't settle for only attending worship services when it's convenient, nor will we approach church with a consumer mindset. We'll dig into the messiness of local church life, opening up our lives to our new spiritual family. Families are messy and costly, but worth it. When we live our lives like we really are spiritual brothers and sisters, it changes everything.

Family is one of the greatest blessings of the gospel. We're never alone. We have family everywhere. We can love and be loved and display God's glory in ways that we never could alone.

5. You Can Have Hope When You Suffer

I've learned to avoid giving easy answers when other people are suffering. It's usually much better to offer friendship, silent companionship, and practical help rather than words.

As I've walked through hard times myself and alongside others, I've discovered three truths that have been of great comfort.

First, it's okay to grieve. I'm grateful the Bible gives us permission to do this. In fact, the book of Psalms contains more songs of lament than any other kind of psalm. There's a time to weep, both for ourselves and with others who are going through difficult times (Rom. 12:15).

Second, we're invited to pray. My prayers in the middle of suffering aren't articulate, but that's okay. As Paul explained in his letter to the Romans, "For we do not know what to pray for as we ought, but the Spirit himself intercedes for us with groanings too deep for words" (Rom. 8:26). God knows what we're saying even when we lack words. And more importantly, He cares.

Finally, I've found it helpful to remember that God is at work even through our suffering. I don't say this lightly, nor do I always understand it, but it's true. This won't erase the pain, but it allows us to rest in the fact that God hasn't lost control. He promises to work everything together for good in this life (Rom. 8:28), and He will wipe every tear from our eyes, and will eliminate death, mourning, and fear (Rev. 21:4). If you, like Sam Gamgee in The Lord of the Rings, wonder "is everything sad going to come untrue?"[8] you're not alone.

We don't always understand what God is doing. "How unsearchable are his judgments and how inscrutable his ways!" exclaims Paul (Rom. 11:33). The gospel doesn't give us the *answers*, but it gives us *assurance* that God hasn't abandoned us.

These truths don't eliminate our tears or short-circuit our grief, but they provide immeasurable comfort. God is so committed to us in Jesus that He has promised to use even the hard things in life for our ultimate good, even if we can't see it at the time.

6. You Can Know Your Life Has Meaning

Recent data indicates that early retirement may lead to a shorter life span.[9] It turns out that we gain economic, social, and other benefits from our work. We thrive when our lives are full of purpose, meaning, and identity.

We're given important tasks that matter for eternity—to make disciples and to use our gifts to serve others.

The gospel is what truly gives us what our souls crave: a deep sense of our innate value and identity. Through the gospel, we become God's own children, His precious possession, His royal priesthood (1 Peter 2:9). We're given important tasks that matter for eternity—to make disciples and to use our gifts to serve others (Matt. 28:18–20; 1 Peter 4:10–11).

I often feel insignificant. When I focus on the fact that I'm one of 7.6 billion people alive on a tiny planet in a vast universe, it doesn't seem to matter how hard I work or what I leave behind. I will be forgotten. A hundred years from now, nobody will even remember that I was alive.

Yet I won't be forgotten by God. I've been adopted by Him. Scripture tells us we matter and none of our work for Him will be wasted (1 Cor. 15:58). We're given an identity that can't be taken away, and our actions matter, not just now but for eternity. We have everything we need to live lives of significance.

7. You Have an Example to Follow

We often learn best by example. The problem with examples is that they can sometimes discourage us. Usain Bolt doesn't encourage me to be a better runner, for instance. He encourages me to give up because no matter how hard I try, I'll never run like him.

If we're not careful, the example of Jesus might dishearten us because we feel we can never measure up. But when we're gripped by what Jesus did for us, His example actually motivates us. I had a hard time forgiving somebody a couple of years ago. Remembering how much Jesus forgave me when I didn't deserve it motivated me to extend forgiveness to that individual (Luke 7:47). It didn't happen instantly or easily, but it happened. The gospel served as an example and motivation at the same time.

Jesus provides an example for us in so many areas. The Bible uses Jesus' actions as a pattern for us, and it also gives us the power to follow this pattern, which we couldn't do on our own. We may not want to be generous, until we consider how generous Jesus has been to us (2 Cor. 8:9). Men may not know how to love their wives, but they learn from and are motivated by the way Jesus treasures the church, His bride (Eph. 5:25–30). When we're mistreated, we can remember that Jesus was mistreated for us (1 Peter 2:21–25). When we see what Jesus did for us, it motivates us to follow His example.

BRINGING THE GOSPEL TO LIFE

The gospel doesn't just bring us into right relationship with God and assure us of our future with Him; it also provides rich resources for dealing with every part of life—our marriages, work lives, relationships, habits, bodies, emotions, and more. It has the power to change every part of our lives from the inside out. There's nothing that it leaves alone.

The gospel isn't just good news that gets us to heaven. It's God Himself, who is in relationship with us, who is transforming us, and who gives us everything that we need.

The gospel isn't just good news that gets us to heaven. It's not even a set of resources or benefits that we get to enjoy. It's God Himself, who is in relationship with us, who is transforming us, and who gives us everything that we need.

The old hymn "How Firm a Foundation, Ye Saints of the Lord" asks the question: "What more can He say than to you He hath said, / who unto the Savior for refuge have fled?" Good question. God hasn't held back. He's lavished believers with benefits through the gospel that we can apply to our lives. The Bible assures us that change is possible as we enjoy the intimacy with God that is ours through the gospel, and as we live off its benefits. We can be transformed by the renewal of our minds (Rom. 12:2).

God has given us untold riches. Paul prayed for the Ephesian believers that they would have "the eyes of your hearts enlightened, that you may know what is the hope to which he has called you, what are the riches of his glorious inheritance in the saints" (Eph. 1:18). This should be our prayer too: that we grow in our knowledge of the riches we have in the gospel, and that we begin to live with the knowledge that all these riches are ours and more.

Fighting shame or feeling guilty? Don't believe the lies. God silences your accuser, and He's reclothed you with the righteousness of Jesus. The final verdict has been spoken over your life, and nothing can change that.

Criticized, justly or unjustly? Worse things could be said about us all, but God knows the worst about us and has chosen to pardon and love us, and the court's been adjourned.

Disappointed by the actions of others, or feeling lonely? You couldn't be more loved than you are in Christ. You have the love of your Father. He exults over you. He sings over you.

Frustrated by your lack of progress? Struggling with negative or damaging patterns of behavior? God is at work in your life. He promises His power. He's changing you from the inside out, and He always finishes what He starts.

Tired of trying to make it on your own? He's given you a family, and that family is everywhere. He invites you to join part of His family near you to display His glory and to love and be loved.

Going through hard times? God knows and God cares. He invites us to grieve, pray, and trust that He's at work even when it's hard. He will one day wipe the tears from our eyes and eliminate death, mourning, and fear (Rev. 21:3–5).

Looking for purpose? God gives us a new identity, meaning, and responsibility. Your life matters because of the gospel. You're now called to faithfully use everything He's given you—your time, body, and more.

Need motivation? The blessings of the gospel motivate us to live lives of worship, gratitude, and service. We've been given an example to follow.

Feeling insecure? The gospel motivates us to stop looking at ourselves and instead look to Jesus, and to begin to put others ahead of us. It gives us the freedom of self-forgetfulness.[10] We'll get to what we must do soon enough. The place to begin, though, is with the good news of what Jesus has done for us.

I started this chapter with the story of Lola, a woman who grew up in slavery. In some ways, Lola's not like us. She did nothing to deserve her slavery. She was a victim. We're culpable in our slavery. We've rebelled against God.

> **The place to begin is with the good news of what Jesus has done for us.**

We are like Lola in one way—we have a hard time accepting our freedom. Once Alex invited Lola to live with him, she continued old behaviors: She threw nothing out. She rifled through the trash to make sure others hadn't thrown out anything useful. She washed and reused paper towels. She kept grocery bags, yogurt containers, and pickle jars. She was free and had everything she needed, yet she continued to live like a poor slave. We're the same. Though we've been set free, we often live like the resources of the gospel aren't ours.

Our greatest problem isn't that we lack freedom. We've been offered freedom and unimaginable wealth through the gospel. Our problem is that we have a hard time living as if it's true.

The key to living like you believe Jesus has freed you from your old identity as a slave is having "the eyes of your hearts enlightened, that you may know what is the hope to which he has called you, what are the riches of his glorious inheritance in the saints, and what is the immeasurable greatness of his power toward us who believe, according to the working of his great might" (Eph. 1:18–19). In other words, we must *accept* what's true and then *live* like it's true.

We'll get to what we must do soon enough. The place to begin, though, is with the good news of what Jesus has *done* for us. Believe it. Celebrate it. This news gives us everything we need to grow.

CHAPTER SUMMARY

- The gospel sets us free, but we tend to continue living like we're slaves.
- The gospel is the good news that God has chosen to rescue His people and the world through the life, death, and resurrection of Jesus.
- The gospel changes everything personally and relationally. It will eventually lead to the renewal of the whole world.
- The gospel gives us immediate benefits when we believe. It also gives us ongoing benefits for all of life.
- The gospel frees us from guilt and shame.
- Because of the gospel and through the gospel, God lavishes us with love. He doesn't tolerate us; He exults over us.
- God transforms us from the inside out. He gives us the

Holy Spirit to change, and promises that He will complete the process of transformation.

- God puts us into community so that we can love and be loved, and display His glory.
- God cares for us in our griefs, uses even our suffering for our good, and will one day undo and banish all that's bad.
- God fills our lives with identity, meaning, and responsibility.
- When we consider what Jesus has done for us, we're motivated to follow His example.
- God gives us even more riches than these. We can pray to know and enjoy more of the blessings He gives us through the gospel.

Questions for Personal Reflection or Group Discussion

1. How would you explain the gospel?
2. What truth about the gospel means the most to you?
3. Why do you think we often treat the gospel as old news rather than the best news ever?
4. This chapter outlines seven things that are true for those who have trusted Jesus. Which of the seven truths means the most to you right now?

What Do I Do Now?

- Pick a truth about the gospel, and spend some time thinking about it. Ask God to allow you to really understand it both intellectually and emotionally.
- Consider whether you have responded to the gospel with repentance and faith. If you haven't, I encourage you to do so today.
- Think about one way your life would change if you really believed the gospel is true. Ask God to begin to make that change happen.
- Pray that you would have "the eyes of your hearts enlightened, that you may know what is the hope to which he has called you, what are the riches of his glorious inheritance in the saints" (Eph. 1:18).

CHAPTER TWO

WE'RE CREATED
TO GROW

In truth there is nothing more thrilling, more solid,
more exhilarating, more humanity-restoring,
more radiantly joyous, than holiness.

DANE ORTLUND, *EDWARDS ON THE CHRISTIAN LIFE*

I've never met a person who doesn't want to grow, nor have I met a person who's satisfied with his or her growth. We feel the tension: we long for growth, but we often feel stuck and apathetic. We can relate to what the author of Hebrews writes: "For though by this time you ought to be teachers, you need someone to teach you again the basic principles of the oracles of God. You need milk, not solid food" (Heb. 5:12). We're not as far along as we thought we'd be.

We understand what Carl Sandburg said: "There is an eagle

in me that wants to soar, and there's a hippopotamus in me that wants to wallow in the mud."[1] Much of the time, the hippopotamus seems to win.

This book is written to help address our desire for growth, along with our frustration that we haven't made as much progress as we'd like. This book isn't just about spiritual growth. We're complex creatures. God made us as humans with bodies, emotions, relationships, minds, and souls. It's impossible to compartmentalize these areas. If I'm stuck in one, it's going to affect the others. If we make progress in one, it will also affect every other area. God cares about all of our lives, so this book is about how to apply the gospel to all of life.

I've read many self-help books, and I'm afraid most of them haven't helped. The label identifies the problem: we can't really help ourselves. We need God to change us, and we need the help of others. Change is possible, but it only comes as we learn about the means God has provided for us to change, and as we slowly and imperfectly place ourselves in the paths of grace. God has promised to meet us there. We're going to explore some of these in the second half of this book.

God made us to grow. It's important to understand what growth is, and the pathway He's designed for growth.

The news is good: we can grow in ways we haven't imagined, and we can help those around us grow too. But we must first learn how to grow, and then begin to practice the habits that will put us in the path of God's grace. This book is designed to help. God made us to grow. It's important to understand what growth is, and the pathway He's designed for growth.

THE CONTEXT: ALL OF LIFE

This book isn't about discipleship the way we normally think about it. Books on discipleship often focus on becoming a better Christian through better quiet times, memorizing Bible verses, learning to pray, and showing up at church. All of this is important—vital, actually—but it's not enough. By contrast, this book is about experiencing transformation in every part of our lives.

The gospel of Luke concludes the childhood years of Jesus with two statements that summarize His early years: "And the child grew and became strong, filled with wisdom. And the favor of God was upon him. . . . And Jesus increased in wisdom and in stature and in favor with God and man" (Luke 2:40, 52). Luke reports that Jesus kept growing in four areas of life:

- **wisdom** (skill in living)
- **stature** (physical growth and health)
- **favor with God** (spiritually)
- **favor with man** (socially)

What's amazing about this is how ordinary and familiar it is. Even Jesus, who is God in the flesh, had to grow. Luke's words echo the story of another child who lived hundreds of years earlier: "Now the boy Samuel continued to grow both in stature and in favor with the LORD and also with man" (1 Sam. 2:26). Although Jesus was unique, He still had to grow by degrees just like the rest of us do. He had to grow physically. He learned a trade. He enjoyed food. He observed rhythms of work and rest. He attended social events such as weddings and funerals. He learned how to pray and how to relate to others. He developed life skills. He didn't live on some spiritual plane detached from reality, but grew as a person in a particular time and place. To be alive as a person means to grow—not just spiritually, but in every dimension of our humanity.

God cares about our minds. As John Stott writes in *Your Mind Matters,* "God has revealed himself in *words* to *minds.* His revelation is a rational revelation to rational creatures."[2] He created us to think, and in creation He gave us a task—creating culture—that requires our mental faculties. Although our mental capacities were damaged by sin, God renews our minds (Rom. 12:2).

God cares about our bodies. I'm always amazed by how physical and sensory the Bible is. We're told about people eating, walking, sleeping, moving to various locations, defecating, fighting, having sex, and more—all very physical things. Even the resurrected Jesus shows up in a body that can be touched, a body that eats. In eternity, we'll have physical, resurrected bodies on the new earth, not disembodied spirits floating on the clouds. We're not souls trapped in a body; we are physical beings. God cares about what we do with our bodies: how we eat, who we sleep with, what we wear, and more. "Do you not know that your body is a temple of the Holy Spirit within you, whom you have from God? You are not your own, for you were bought with a price. So glorify God in your body" (1 Cor. 6:19–20).

> **To be alive as a person means to grow—not just spiritually, but in every dimension of our humanity.**

God cares about our relationships. Jesus modeled this: He enjoyed a network of friends and is frequently found visiting homes and sharing meals. Many of the New Testament letters outline in detail how we're to act within the context of our various relationships: the church, those who are skeptical about Jesus, as well as our friends and families.

God cares about our work, which is a good thing, considering many of us will spend more than sixty thousand hours on the job throughout the course of our life. Rather than working just to survive, our work fulfills God's mandate to Adam and Eve to fill and subdue the earth, and to bring order out of chaos (Gen. 1:28; 2:15)—and as a form of worship and love. The gospel brings meaning to our work, even work that seems mundane.[3] "Whatever you do, work heartily, as for the Lord and not for men, knowing that from the Lord you will receive the inheritance as your reward. You are serving the Lord Christ" (Col. 3:23–24).

We need what Tish Harrison Warren calls a liturgy of the ordinary: a sense of God's presence in every part of our ordinary life.[4] Paul writes in his letter to the Colossians, "Whatever you do, in word or deed, do everything in the name of the Lord Jesus, giving thanks to God the Father through him" (Col. 3:17). That's what I'm interested in. "Whether you eat or drink, or whatever you do, do all to the glory of God" (1 Cor. 10:31).

WHAT GROWTH ISN'T

Sometimes we get confused about what growth is. Because of this, we may end up failing because we've succeeded at the wrong goal. Here are some things that growth isn't.

Growth isn't self-help. By self-help, I mean the idea that we can find the resources we need to change within ourselves. The Bible never presents spiritual maturity and growth as something we can bring about solely through our own efforts. As Jared C. Wilson writes in *The Imperfect Disciple,* "Do you know why there are a thousand fresh self-help books every year? It's because they don't work. We keep looking for the answer within us, as if we'll find it in the same place as the problems. Self-help is like sticking your broken hand in the blender, thinking that'll fix it."[5] We can't help ourselves because our problems run far too deep. And the issue isn't just that we do bad things; it's that we're enslaved to sin. Because of the Fall, we're predisposed to act out of self-serving motives and we can't overcome this tendency on our own. We need a power outside of ourselves to change us and set us free, and this power is only found in the gospel.

Many of our approaches to spiritual growth assume too much about our ability to affect change ourselves. Instead of self-help, our hope rests in the fact that God's divine power "has granted to us all things that pertain to life and godliness, through the knowledge of him who called us to his own glory and excellence" (2 Peter 1:3). Any attempts to grow apart from God are doomed to fail.

Growth isn't just more information. Sometimes we assume people just need to *know* more in order to experience growth. To be sure, knowledge is important. Scripture teaches us about God, and it's critical that we know more about Him. We need what Scripture teaches us in order to grow (2 Tim. 3:15–17). But knowledge isn't enough. The apostle Paul himself recognized that knowledge can make us more arrogant (1 Cor. 8:1). Many of us know a lot about God, but it hasn't always translated into greater holiness. We need more than another workbook or curriculum. Knowledge is essential, but it's not enough.

Growth isn't about the latest program. We're sometimes tempted to think that we need a new book or product if we're going to grow. Entire industries are built on revealing the missing keys that have been holding you back—the secret key to unlocking our greatness. We don't need a new approach, or newly discovered knowledge, though. We need to rediscover something that's existed for generations, and must be continually discovered and reapplied. We don't need something new; we need something old that we're likely to overlook.

Growth isn't about behavioral modification. Growth isn't about changing our behavior or controlling ourselves when we're tempted to sin. It goes much deeper. It gets to the very core of who we are: our heart. It is, as Dallas Willard put it, a renovation of the heart.[6] We miss out if we settle for merely acting differently, if it's not flowing from inner transformation. God wants to accomplish much more in us.

So, go beyond self-help. Don't be content with seeking information, a new approach, or superficial change. Don't settle for less than God desires. It's tragic when we succeed at the wrong goal. Our goal in growth must be nothing less than what God intends for us.

WHAT GROWTH IS

According to the *Westminster Shorter Catechism*, sanctification—another word for the kind of growth we're talking about—is: "the work of God's free grace, whereby we are renewed in the *whole man* after the image of God, and are enabled more and more to die unto sin, and live unto righteousness."[7] J. I. Packer provides a helpful clarification, "The concept is not of sin being totally eradicated (that is to claim too much) or merely counteracted (that is to say too little), but of a divinely wrought character change freeing us from sinful habits and forming in us Christlike affections, dispositions, and virtues."[8] With that in mind, here are the hallmarks of authentic spiritual growth.

Growth takes place by God's grace. We don't grow on our own. We can't just pull ourselves up by our own bootstraps. God promises us His Spirit to transform us from the inside out.

Growth is for all of life. God changes every part of us; the gospel applies to every part of life. It's just as relevant for our recreation, leisure, relationships, physical health and wellness, as it is for our devotional and church lives.

Growth isn't about us. Don't get me wrong: growth changes us, but it's not *about* us. It will increase our joy and transform us. But growth is about love for God and others. Growth helps us to love God and others in the everyday realities of our complicated lives.

Growth transforms us into Christ's image. God made us in His image; that image has been tarnished by sin, but has not been destroyed. God works in us to restore that image and to make us who God designed us to be.

> **Growth changes us, but it's not about us. It will increase our joy and transform us. But growth is about love for God and others.**

Growth frees us from sin and to righteousness. God sets us free from our greatest problem, and changes us from the inside out so that we can live for Him.

Growth is about habits and desire. Growth isn't abstract. It is revealed by the things and activities we choose to invest ourselves in. As James K. A. Smith says, we are what we love.[9] It also shows up in our habits: the daily practices that make us who we are.

So often we think the Christian life is just about forgiveness of our sins, losing sight of God's plan to completely transform us. We settle for an impoverished vision of growth in one or two areas of life, when God's desire is to reign over every part. We believe growth is up to us, forgetting that the Spirit dwells within us. We think of sanctification in lofty, abstract terms, neglecting to translate it into the rhythms of our moments and days. Jeff Vanderstelt captures what a comprehensive picture of spiritual growth looks like:

> It is the ongoing process of submitting all of life to Jesus, and seeing him saturate your entire life and world with his presence and power. It's a process of daily growing in your awareness of your need for him in the everyday stuff of life. It is walking with Jesus, being filled with Jesus, and being led by Jesus in every place and in every way.[10]

This is what I want to tackle in this book. More than that though, I want to describe the practical steps we can take to grow spiritually and in every other area of our lives.

OUR INTERCONNECTED LIVES

My wife, Charlene, spoke to me recently about the growth she's seen in her life over the past five years. She's always been insightful and caring, and I love that she pursues God with honesty and tenderness. But in the last five years, she grew in a way we didn't expect: through a fitness and nutrition program. Charlene has become healthier physically and she's also developed more emotional resilience. In the process, she's also grown in her walk with God and in her relationship with others. Her recent growth wasn't because she doubled down on spiritual disciplines. It began as she pursued habits of physical wellbeing—healthy eating, increased movement and exercise, a daily sleep routine—which affected all of the other areas of her life. She writes,

> When my weight was excessive I thought of stewardship in spiritual and relational terms. I made no connections between my habits of haphazard sleep, skipping meals, and lack of physical movement to "what mattered most" spiritually.
>
> One of my first spiritual connections came when I was required to practice the habit of a sleep routine. While I already had a practice of Sabbath, now I began to look at the quality of my physical, daily rest. Inconsistent evening activities resulted in frequent nights of too little sleep followed by days and nights of too much sleep. As I pursued greater consistency in my hours of sleep I learned to support my goal of a good

night's sleep by developing a sleep routine—limiting electronics and media after 9:00 pm, communicating my evening plans to others in my home, turning down the lights, getting ready for bed—a pattern of signals and cues to prepare my body for rest. As I practiced these behaviors, I gained an increasing awareness of the connection between evening and morning—my bodily lived experience aligned more fully with the pattern of Genesis—evening and morning together form a day.

Experiencing biblical images and phrases come alive physically continued as I pursued physical well-being. In the winter of 2015 a friend encouraged me to try a triathlon just for fun. The New Testament's comparison of spiritual growth to athletic training, competing within the race boundaries, the joy of crossing the finish line, hearing your name called to the cheers of the crowd, to finish the course, the winner crowned, these words moved from thought to physical reality. Alive in experience, these words of scripture forever change my relating to and embracing of these Scriptures.

As I progressed with developing habits for physical health and wellbeing, the connection between my physical body and spiritual and emotional health began to increase. The benefits of eating healthy foods slowly, increased exercise and better rest, contributed to measurable improvements in my health and noticeable positive impacts on my emotional resilience and mood. The Lord was redeeming my body, mind and soul into a more complete expression of what he created it to be.[11]

Don't get me wrong. I'm not saying a healthy diet and workout routine will automatically result in a healthy soul. But the various components of our lives are interconnected, and, as God deals with one part of our lives it affects all the others. As we submit one part of our life to God and live in His power, we'll see growth in every part of life. God wants to renovate your entire life, beginning with the deepest parts of you.

LET'S COMMIT TO GROWTH

So let's commit to growth. Discipling others and growing in spiritual maturity ourselves—these tasks lie at the very heart of our mission as believers. We must grow. It's God's intent for each of us. You were made to grow. Not only that, but you *can* grow. God has given us means by which we can experience His grace and be transformed. Best of all, He hasn't left us alone. He's given us His Spirit and His people to help us to grow. So let's pursue growth, for ourselves and for our churches. You were made for this.

In the next chapter, we're going to examine what growth looks like. It's a much richer, more complex picture than what we usually imagine. Then, in later chapters, we're going to explore where to start, and the practical steps you can take to grow. Finally, we'll look at how to help others grow too.

CHAPTER SUMMARY

- We were made to desire growth.
- We're meant to grow in every part of life: in our minds, bodies, work, and our relationship with God and others.
- Growth isn't self-help, accumulating more information, looking for a new approach, or behavioral modification.

- Growth is the renewal of every part of our lives by God's grace. It transforms us into God's image, frees us from sin, and involves our habits and desires.
- By God's grace, growth is possible.

Questions for Personal Reflection or Group Discussion

1. When is a time that you have experienced growth? What factors do you think led to that growth?
2. Why do you think that we sometimes believe that God is only interested in our spiritual lives?
3. In which area of your life—intellectual, physical, mental, relational, spiritual—do you want to grow most?
4. "Growth is the renewal of every part of our lives by God's grace. It transforms us into God's image, frees us from sin, and involves our habits and desires." What do you think of this understanding of growth?
5. In what ways do you hope to grow in the coming year?

What Do I Do Now?

- Do a quick assessment of the various areas of your life: intellectual, physical, mental, relational, and spiritual. Think about how you would like to grow in each of these areas. (Visit https://gospelforlife.com/assessment for a quick assessment tool.)
- Spend some time praying about each of these areas. Acknowledge that you need God's help. Commit each of these areas to God.

CHAPTER THREE

RETHINKING GROWTH: PURSUING JOY AND TRANSFORMED DESIRES

The happiest state of a Christian is the holiest state.
CHARLES H. SPURGEON, *MORNING AND EVENING*

Imagine if our churches were known for being communities of Jesus-centered happiness, overflowing with the sheer gladness of what it means to live out the good news of great joy. . . . Wouldn't this infuse the gospel with a meaning that most of the world has never heard and that even many of God's people have never known?
RANDY ALCORN, *HAPPINESS*

I grew up in a church that took God seriously. We were allowed to have fun, but when it came time to talk about God, the fun ended. I began to develop the idea that spiritual maturity means we should become increasingly serious. Spiritual giants, I thought, smile less and frown more. I had completely missed a major theme of Scripture, and the entire point of spiritual maturity.

I also thought that spiritual maturity was otherworldly. I thought it meant caring less about ordinary life: parenting, working, playing, resting. I seemed to think that the more holy a person was, the less human they were.

My image of spiritual maturity couldn't have been uglier: serious, otherworldly, and less concerned with everyday life. It's not a pretty picture, nor is it the biblical picture of growth.

Looking back, I had three wrong beliefs about growth:

1. Spiritual growth is about becoming less human.
2. Spiritual growth involves becoming more serious.
3. Spiritual growth involves denying my desires.

These three ideas made spiritual growth unattractive to me. I guess I still wanted it because it's the right thing to do, but I didn't expect it to be much fun.

I couldn't have been more wrong. Spiritual maturity isn't about white-knuckling it to sainthood. It's about becoming a person who is fully alive. It means enjoying God and life in deeper and more abundant ways even in the middle of difficulty. It tranforms our desires rather than denying them. Spiritual growth is the pursuit of God, and the pursuit of joy. It's the happiest and best way to live.

THE OPPOSITE OF SPIRITUAL GROWTH

To be honest, it's easier to think of sin as fun and spiritual growth as unpleasant. We think the sinners get to live it up, while the godly live boring, dutiful lives.

For sure, sin can be fun. But the fun is shortlived and ultimately destructive. It never delivers what it promises. Sin promises the good life but never delivers on the joy it dangles before us.

According to the Bible, sin is corrosive, and it destroys everything that it touches. Sin kills. Our sinful desires wage war against our souls (1 Peter 2:11). Sin "interferes with the way things are supposed to be," writes Cornelius Plantinga.[1] It has destroyed the conditions of flourishing that God designed for the world and everyone in it.

The beginning of Scripture introduces us to a good world created by God. By chapter 3 of Genesis, humanity rebels against God, resulting in broken human relationships, a loss of intimacy with God, difficulty and aggravation in carrying out our roles, physical death, and more. The next chapters of the Bible illustrate how quickly things fall apart. It's a depressing but realistic depiction of the effects of sin on us and our world. The fallout was extensive. Sin corrupted everything, beginning with us and extending to our relationships, our bodies, our work, and nature itself. Nothing is the way it's supposed to be.

Sin promises what it can never deliver. It always lies. It's enticing because we think that it will give us what we want, but it always leaves us unsatisfied. Even worse, it destroys everything that it touches.

We were made to grow and flourish, but sin has led to the loss of the world we want to live in.

Spiritual growth is the opposite. It doesn't destroy; it gives life. God is in the business of restoring our humanity, giving us more joy, and renovating our desires.

RESTORING HUMANITY

Spiritual growth isn't about becoming less human. It's about God restoring us and the world to what it should be.

I used to think that God cared about certain things—prayer, pastors, and church—but I couldn't figure out what God thought about the rest of life. *Are we supposed to endure most of life so that we could get to the important parts on Sunday?* I wondered. It seemed like spiritual growth didn't have much to do with going to school, paying bills, working, or parenting. God was a part of my life—the most important part—and then there was everything else.

One day I read a sentence from a monk named Brother Lawrence who served in a monastery in the 1600s: "I flip my little omelette in the frying pan for the love of God."[2] This startled me. He didn't seem to see a difference between ordinary things like cooking and God. His whole life mattered to God.

> *God doesn't want us to separate our spiritual growth from the rest of life; He wants it all.*

I began to notice how much of the Bible is about ordinary life: eating, working, marriage, and parenting. I learned that God cares about the world—not just church, but everything. God doesn't want us to separate our spiritual growth from the rest of life; He wants it all.

I also began to learn that God cares so much about this world that He plans to restore it. I was once asked to speak to a classroom of young children about heaven. I spoke of gates of pearl and streets of gold. The children pressed me: what will life be like there? I couldn't tell them. Frankly, heaven didn't sound exciting to me when it sounded otherworldly. I pictured choirs and clouds. Beyond that, I had no ideas, except that it didn't sound fun.

I'd missed that our future isn't heaven, but rather heaven coming to earth. "Then I saw a new heaven and a new earth, for the first heaven and the first earth had passed away, and the sea was no more," John writes in Revelation. "And I saw the holy city, new Jerusalem, coming down out of heaven from God, prepared as a bride adorned for her husband" (Rev. 21:1–2). Best of all, God will come to live with us. "And I heard a loud voice from the throne saying, 'Behold, the dwelling place of God is with man. He will dwell with them, and they will be his people, and God himself will be with them as their God'" (Rev. 21:3). I'd also forgotten about our resurrection bodies. We won't escape living in our bodies on this earth; instead, we'll finally enjoy living on the earth as humans the way that God intended.

Spiritual growth isn't about an escape from this world. It's about recovering who we were meant to be in this world, longing for and praying for the restoration of all things.

I began to realize that God cares deeply about this world right now. Even more, He cares about us. God's intent for us is the restoration of all things, including our humanity. Sin began with individuals and spread like a disease throughout the world. Similarly, God restores the world first by restoring individuals, but He intends to do more. He will one day restore everything. The world will once again be what He intended in the first place, only better.

This earth matters. We're meant to enjoy it. Some may sing that the world is not their home, and they're just passing through. I know what they mean, but they're wrong. Earth—one day the new earth—is exactly where God intends for us to be. God doesn't plan to snatch us away from earth to live in heaven forever. His plan is that we would live, in our resurrected bodies, in His restored world, with His presence. God's plan isn't to destroy the world so we can escape it; it's to recreate the world so that we can live with it. We're designed to be worldly saints.[3]

Spiritual growth isn't about an escape from this world. It's about recovering who we were meant to be in this world, longing for and praying for the restoration of all things. It's about becoming more human as we move closer to God's original intent for humanity in this world.

God cares about every part of our lives. He's not just interested in what we do at church on Sundays. He cares about who we are at school and work, in our homes and cars, in coffee shops and restaurants and every moment of our day-to-day lives. There's no such thing as a Christian life that is detached from our recreational, mundane, or work life. All of it belongs to Him. And the purpose of our lives isn't for us to become otherworldly; it's for us to flourish as humans in the world that God has created. It's also to fulfill our roles within this world: to love God, serve others, cultivate the earth through our work, and rest.

I love that picture of spiritual growth a lot more than the one I used to hold. God cares about our lives, and He cares about this world. He's restoring our lives, and He's going to one day restore the world so that it's what He meant it to be.

Spiritual growth is about all of life.

RESTORING JOY

God doesn't just want to restore our humanity. He also wants to restore our joy. He's so committed to our joy that I don't know how I ever got the idea that God is a killjoy.

I grew up thinking that God tolerated our joy; I've since discovered that it's at the heart of what God intends for us. Psalm 16:11 says:

> You make known to me the path of life;
> in your presence there is fullness of joy;
> at your right hand are pleasures forevermore.

This theme repeats itself throughout Scripture. Psalm 4:7 says,

"You have put more joy in my heart than they have when their grain and wine abound." When God's people returned to Jerusalem after exile, Nehemiah and Ezra told them, "Do not be grieved, for the joy of the LORD is your strength" (Neh. 8:10). The growth of the early church in the book of Acts is portrayed as the spread of joy (Acts 8:8). Before going to the cross, Jesus told His followers, "These things I have spoken to you, that my joy may be in you, and that your joy may be full" (John 15:11).

I used to read verses like this, and not know what to do with them. They were like puzzle pieces that didn't fit with my picture of God or the Christian life. I remember being staggered by the first question of the Westminster Shorter Catechism:

Q: What is the chief end of man?
A: Man's chief end is to glorify God, and to enjoy him forever.[4]

The first part of the answer made sense to me. Glorify God? I agreed with that part. Enjoy Him forever? It seemed selfish to me. I seemed to think that holiness and joy have an inverse relationship. The more holiness, the less joy. The more joy, the less holiness.

It was only later that I discovered that holiness and joy belong together. I began to read theologian after theologian argue that God intends to restore our joy.[5] Joy isn't peripheral to what God desires for us. Contrary to what many think, it's at the heart of His design, and it's central to our growth. As C. S. Lewis quipped, "Joy is the serious business of heaven."[6]

Even then, I wondered if joy is something different from happiness. Maybe God wants us to be joyful, but that's something different than being happy, I thought. But then I read Randy Alcorn, author of *Happiness*. He has studied Scripture and church history, and has concluded that the distinction that some make between happiness and joy is unfounded. "I'm convinced that no biblical or historical basis exists to define happiness as inherently sinful," he writes.[7] Elsewhere in the book he says,

> Modern distinctions between happiness and joy are completely counterintuitive. . . . For too long we've distanced the gospel from what . . . God created us to desire—and what he desires for us—happiness. . . .
>
> We need to reverse the trend. Let's redeem the word *happiness* in light of both Scripture and church history. Our message shouldn't be "Don't seek happiness," but "You'll find in Jesus the happiness you've always longed for."[8]

God desires our happiness *and* our holiness. Our problem is that we think that happiness is living life *our* way. We resist God's way of holiness because it seems too constraining and uncomfortable, and then we wonder why we're not as happy as we expected.

To pursue God is to pursue happiness. In the end, the pursuit of God and the pursuit of happiness are the same thing. There is nothing more satisfying than God.

Ironically, we don't find happiness by seeking it. We find happiness by seeking God. We also don't get happiness on our own terms. Satan tempted Jesus with the "perfect" life, with resources, power, and approval—but on his terms. These are the same temptations that Satan has been dangling before us for centuries. Jesus passed the test we fail. He showed us that the good life is found by following a different path: "For whoever would save his life will lose it, but whoever loses his life for my sake and the gospel's will save it" (Mark 8:35). His obedience is credited to us, and He gives us His example to follow. We don't find happiness by pursuing it; we find happiness by abandoning our lives in the pursuit of God. Paradoxically, the happiest husbands are the ones who pursue the happiness of their wives. The happiest leaders are more concerned with serving others than their status or position. The happiest Christians are those who have stopped living for themselves because they're consumed with how they can serve and love Jesus.

Enjoy your life. Savor your food; cheer when your team wins; laugh with your friends; go for a walk and enjoy the fresh air. "There is nothing better for a person than that he should eat and

> *To pursue God is to pursue happiness. In the end, the pursuit of God and the pursuit of happiness are the same thing. There is nothing more satisfying than God.*

drink and find enjoyment in his toil. This also, I saw, is from the hand of God, for apart from him who can eat or who can have enjoyment?" (Eccl. 2:24–25).

As you enjoy these things, treasure God as your greatest joy. When we live for Him, He allows us to enjoy His gifts in this world while holding on to the only lasting source of joy that will sustain us through difficulty. We can best enjoy this world's blessings when we're not living for them, but when we're living for God instead.

TRANSFORMING DESIRES

Our desires lie at the core of our being. Simply put, we want. We're desiring creatures. Every action we take is shaped by our pursuit of what we want.

The Bible is clear about this. It traces our actions, good and bad, to our hearts, the motivational center of our being. "Keep your heart with all vigilance, for from it flow the springs of life" (Prov. 4:23). Jesus diagnosed our problem: "For out of the heart come evil thoughts, murder, adultery, sexual immorality, theft, false witness, slander" (Matt. 15:19). Our problem isn't behavior. Our problem is a heart that wants the wrong thing.

The theme of desire runs through the entire Bible. God, who gave His people His law as an act of grace, told Moses that the people would never be able to keep the law, even after all that He'd done for them. "For I know what they are inclined to do even to-day, before I have brought them into the land that I swore to give," God told him (Deut. 31:21). Even after God had delivered them, they still wanted to do their own thing. Later, God promised to solve this problem by changing hearts:

> "And I will give them one heart, and a new spirit I
> will put within them. I will remove the heart of stone
> from their flesh and give them a heart of flesh, that
> they may walk in my statutes and keep my rules and
> obey them. And they shall be my people, and I will
> be their God." (Ezek. 11:19–20)

Until God gives them a new heart, it will be impossible for them to obey. Once God gives His people a new heart, they'll *want* to obey. God promises to write the law on their hearts, so that everyone, from the least to the greatest, knows Him (Jer. 31:33).

God isn't interested in grudging obedience motivated by guilt or obligation. He isn't interested in external compliance or religious performance. He wants us to want Him sincerely. He wants our complete and unreserved love (Matt. 22:37–40). He makes this possible by changing us, by giving us new hearts. What God wants most is for us to want Him.

We often set our sights too low. When we aim for growth, we often settle for more knowledge. Of course, knowledge is essential. Jesus, after all, included teaching in His final commission to us (Matt. 28:18–20). We must learn the contours of the gospel story, mastering all that God has revealed to us. But we should not only learn facts and stories; we must be mastered by the biblical story so that it becomes *our* story. Knowledge is essential, but it's not enough.

Sometimes we settle for the outward markers that show that we take God seriously, such as church attendance and moral behavior. I once met a man who had been asked to become a deacon at the church he attended. "But I'm an atheist!" he replied. He attended church out of loyalty to his wife. People mistook his faithful attendance and moral life as a sign of his commitment to God. Obedience, like knowledge, is important. In His commission, Jesus told us to teach people "to observe all that I have commanded you" (Matt. 28:20). Both teaching and obedience are essential. They're just not enough.

> *We should not only learn facts and stories; we must be mastered by the biblical story so that it becomes our story.*

The real goal of growth is that our hearts are changed so that we love God more than anything or anyone else, and love the things that He loves. Someone asked Jesus which of the 613 commands in the Hebrew Scriptures is most important. He answered with a commandment that speaks to our desires:

> "You shall love the Lord your God with all your heart and with all your soul and with all your mind. This is the great and first commandment. And a second is like it: You shall love your neighbor as yourself. On these two commandments depend all the Law and the Prophets." (Matt. 22:37–40)

Jesus clears the clutter and gets to the heart. All the commands matter, but none matter more than these: to love God and to love neighbor. If we do these, keeping the rest of the commandments won't be a problem. Change must take place at the level of what we love and want.

God wants nothing less than to change our desires. He doesn't want us only to think differently or behave differently; He wants us to *want* differently because He understands that our behavior and thoughts flow from our desires. In the end, this is the goal of growth.

RETHINKING GROWTH

Our views of growth are often too small. We think about learning more and changing our behavior. Growth isn't less than that, but it's much more. God wants to restore us and to give us joy. The happiest people, it turns out, are the holiest people. He wants us to change our desires.

Our plan for growth must take this into account. If we needed only to learn, we could simply go through a class or read a book. If we only needed to change behavior, we could apply behavioral modification techniques or try to build up our willpower. We'd be frustrated, though, because we could never learn enough or manage our behavior well enough to be satisfied.

We need more than knowledge or behavior change. We need a change of heart. God has given us exactly what we need. In Jesus, we not only have a new heart but the power to change.

God cares about all of our lives: our minds, bodies, work, and our relationships with Him and others. It's about bringing every part of our life under God's control. He doesn't want to make us more serious and otherworldly. He wants us to flourish and become more joyful in our humanity. He wants to change us at the deepest levels so that we don't just think and act differently, but we *want* differently.

I find this whole-life, robust, heart-shaping, eternity-encompassing view of growth to be compelling, and I hope you do too.

Let's not settle for anything less. Let's set our goal on becoming who God wants us to be, by His grace and through His strength.

CHAPTER SUMMARY

- Sin promises joy, but it never delivers. It corrodes everything it touches.
- God is restoring everything. His restoration plan includes the entire world. We're meant to live as restored humans on a restored earth.
- Joy isn't an optional extra. It is central to God's design for us.
- Pursuing God's glory and pursuing our own happiness are the same thing.
- The Christian life is about an increase of desire for and delight in God.
- God gives us new hearts so that we can desire Him rightly.
- God doesn't make cosmetic changes in our lives. He is working to completely change us, including our desires.

Questions for Personal Reflection or Group Discussion

1. "Spiritual maturity isn't about white-knuckling it to sainthood. It's about becoming a person who is fully alive." Is this different from the way you usually think about spiritual maturity?
2. Do you typically see joy and happiness as central to the Christian life? Why or why not?
3. God plans for us to live as restored humans in a restored earth. We're meant to flourish as humans, not escape the earth or our humanity. How is this different from the way you think of the afterlife?

4. Why are we tempted to think God wants to take away rather than increase our joy?

5. How would things change if Christians and churches were known for their joy?

6. Why do you think that we sometimes see desire as a bad thing?

7. Why do you think God wants to change our desires, not just our knowledge or behavior?

What Do I Do Now?

- Make a list of some of the ways that you try to find joy, including the ways that don't work.
- "The happiest Christians are those who have stopped living for themselves because they're consumed with how they can serve and love Jesus." Think of ways that you can focus on pleasing Jesus today rather than focusing on yourself.
- Ask God to give you joy as you pursue Him, and a peace that surpasses understanding even in the middle of your struggles.
- Make a list of some of the desires that motivate your life.
- Journal about the desires that you experience that can ultimately only be satisfied in God.
- Pray for the type of growth we've looked at: that it would affect all of your life, make you more joyful, and transform your desires.

CHAPTER FOUR

KNOW WHERE YOU ARE, THEN TAKE THE NEXT STEP

There are no experts in the company of Jesus.
We are all beginners.
EUGENE PETERSON, *THE JESUS WAY*

I hate shopping malls. My idea of shopping is to visit Amazon, research options for five minutes or less, place my order, and then pick up the package at the front desk of my condo a few days later. Visiting a shopping mall is about as fun for me as a trip to the dentist. Occasionally, though, I find myself in a gargantuan mall. Inevitably I get lost and I'm forced to do one of three things: find an information desk, locate a map display, or open the mall app on my phone. In order to get where I need to go, I first need to find out where I am.

"You are here" turns out to be one of the most helpful markers in any exploration. To get to our ultimate destination, we all need to begin where we are.

BEGIN WHERE YOU ARE

We're currently teaching our eighteen-year-old son how to drive standard. He's new to driving, and he's new to driving a car with a manual transmission. He gets frustrated when he stalls the car or when it lurches. He watches us and can't understand why he's having such a hard time when we aren't.

He doesn't know that I learned how to use a clutch in Vancouver, a city of hills. I remember being stopped at a red light on a hill with a car behind me and praying that I would be able get into first gear instead of sliding back into his car. It wasn't pretty, but I learned quickly. He also doesn't remember my wife's early attempts at driving standard, which coincided with my early attempts to be a more patient husband. Everybody struggles at first.

It's the same, of course, with God. Eugene Peterson calls discipleship a long obedience in the same direction.[1] Discipleship takes time.

When I took a running course, I was anxious to progress quickly. I found 5K runs pretty easy, and set my sights on 10Ks and half-marathons. It's a classic mistake. I first had to put in the hours building a foundation. Then I could slowly add mileage and intensity, but only at a controlled rate. Progressing too quickly would lead to injury and burnout. Until the foundation is in place, healthy progression is impossible.

It's the same in our growth. We're often eager to progress. But first, we must understand where we are, and build a foundation that will help us take the next step in our growth.

Assessments are helpful in many areas of life. Our financial planner regularly asks us to rate our investment knowledge (and my wife, Charlene, always rates higher). When taking a course, instructors often begin by assessing the current knowledge of students. Health professionals regularly hand me a clipboard with questions that assess every conceivable health question. Personal trainers always begin with assessing the fitness of new clients.

Somehow we don't often assess ourselves spiritually. We sometimes treat ourselves and others as if we're all at the same level, or that the length of time we've been a Christian says something about our spiritual maturity. The apostle Paul wrote, "Examine yourselves, to see whether you are in the faith. Test yourselves" (2 Cor. 13:5). Paul tells the Corinthians that their response to an upcoming visit will be a test of the legitimacy of their faith. "Let each one test his own work," he advised the church in Galatia (Gal. 6:4).

Charles Simeon, a pastor in Cambridge, England, from the nineteenth century, was right:

> Self-knowledge is at the root of all true religion.
> Without that, we shall have no right disposition, either
> towards God or man. . . . To cultivate self-knowledge
> therefore is, in this view, extremely important: but
> more especially is it so in the prospect of that judg-
> ment which God himself will shortly pass on every
> child of man: for, whatever be our estimate of our own
> character, it is not by that, but by God's own view of us,
> that our state shall be determined to all eternity.[2]

We must begin by knowing ourselves and where we are right now.

As we grow, it also helps to assess where we are, so that we can take the appropriate steps to progress to the next stage and be encouraged by the progress we've already made. As in running, we need to build the proper foundation that will allow us to progress to maturity and avoid unrealistic expectations.

PICTURING GROWTH

Growth is never neat or linear. We like to categorize people and to describe clear, discreet steps in growth. We're more complicated than this. Any attempt to describe growth will fail to capture the realities of what takes place in the lives of real, complicated people.

Nevertheless, it's helpful to have a picture of growth. For one thing, it helps us understand the normal progression that people take as they grow to maturity. It also helps us understand what's realistic at each stage, what to expect, and how to take the next step.

The model below is derived from a few different sources:[3]

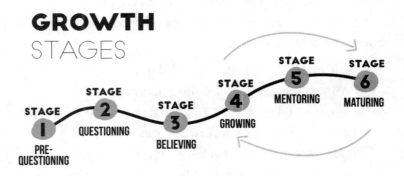

GROWTH
STAGES

As you can see, there are six stages on the path to maturity. Each stage is broad enough to cover a series of sub-stages. These stages focus primarily on where we are in relationship to God as we think about how to bring every part of our lives under His control. Although God cares about every part of our lives, we'll never grow as He designs until we submit to His rule and tap into the transforming power of the gospel.

Stage One: Pre-Questioning

This stage is the most common, especially in our post-Christian culture. Some are glad that Christianity works for some people, but they see it as one of many options that they can choose from. Others even see it as a harmful option. They're hostile toward religious institutions, and don't see faith as a viable option or as good for society. They don't think that Jesus could have anything to do with them.

If you're reading this book, I'm guessing that you're not at this stage. Most people who fit this stage wouldn't pick up a book like this, and probably wouldn't make it this far.

If you do fit in this stage, though, you're not alone. An increasing number of people in the West identify as religiously unaffiliated, including many who in past generations may have self-identified as Christian or as part of some other religious group. They don't identify as religious, don't attend a church or any other religious group, and in general are uninterested in religion.

A person who is Pre-Questioning might say, "I'm convinced of a different truth, generally skeptical, or completely focused on other things in life. I have no real interest in Jesus and his message." They may even express hostility to Christianity.

To become a questioner, the Pre-Questioning need stimulating conversations, genuine friendship with a Christian, to see a provocative Christian lifestyle, and to be asked good questions. Most people who move to the next stage do so as a result of relationships or a crisis.

Stage Two: Questioning

I met her at a board-game group in our community. She learned that I was a pastor, which usually leads to a raised eyebrow or two. We continued to play games and talk. I didn't think she was interested in faith. A while later, though, she wanted to meet me for coffee. She was curious about God, and she had questions. She was Questioning.

There are people who are curious about Jesus. They may not know much about Christianity, but they're open. Often, something's happened in their life—a transition or a traumatic event—to make them more interested. They have questions. How can they know what's true? Why Jesus? They may also have questions about specific Christian beliefs. They want to learn more.

Almost everyone in the Bible who believed was at this stage, or got there quickly. It's a treat to meet someone who is Questioning. It's usually clear that God is at work in their life.

If you're Questioning, you're in a good position. You're interested in Jesus. You have lots of questions. You're not quite sold on Christianity, but you're open.

If that's you, then there are some steps you can take. First, I encourage you to explore the story of Christianity. It's a grand story, and a beautiful one. Books like *The Story of Reality* by Greg Koukl and *The Big Story* by Justin Buzzard provide a good introduction to the story. They help us understand what C. S. Lewis meant when he said, "I believe in Christianity as I believe that the sun has risen: not only because I see it, but because by it I see everything else."[4] As we begin to understand the story of Christianity, it becomes our story. We begin to see it as the story that makes sense of the world.

Of course, you can always dive into the Bible. I usually don't recommend that you start at the beginning if you're new to the Bible, but some brave people ignore my advice and survive. There are so many good study tools available today that, with hard work and a bit of grit, you can make sense of the parts of the Bible that are hard to understand.

For most people, though, I recommend starting in a part of the

Bible that's more accessible. Pick one of the Gospels (the books that tell us about the life of Jesus)—Matthew, Mark, Luke, or John—and begin there. Pay attention to Jesus. Whenever I read the Gospels, I'm reminded of how different He is than what we expect. There's no one quite like Him.

Of course, it helps to explore Christianity with others. One of the most powerful ways to experience Christianity is to find a group of Christians and see how the gospel changes real, imperfect people. We're going to cover how to find a good church in chapter 7. For now, let me encourage you to find a church in which the Bible is opened regularly, the main subject is Jesus, and where members talk more about what Jesus has done than about what we need to do. There are other good things to look for, but if the church takes the gospel seriously and welcomes you and your questions, that's a good start.

One of the beautiful things about Christian community is that it's messy. I love watching ordinary people bump against each other with their quirks and questions. It's awkward, but it's beautiful. Don't look for a polished church in which everyone has it together. In fact, run from that church! Look for a church community that allows people to struggle, and where there's evidence that the gospel helps people in the middle of real problems. Watch how Jesus changes people who are working to stay in tune with Jesus, and who then find themselves in tune with others who follow Jesus too.

Begin to explore the story of Christianity in all its contours. Get to know the Bible. Focus on Jesus, who's very compelling. Join a messy church community in which you can observe the difference that Jesus makes with real people. Take a risk. Talk to God. Be honest about your questions. Encourage your curiosity. Let it drive you to Jesus.

Stage Three: Believing

At some point, hopefully questioners make a commitment to Christ and become believers. Believers understand the claims of the gospel. They don't yet have a full understanding of Christianity, and don't always feel comfortable reading the Bible or praying. They are very dependent on others for their spiritual growth. Some desire to grow; some stay stuck here. This is the stage of repentance and trust. Repentance means that we change directions: we turn away from our old ways of thinking and living, and we turn to Jesus. It means we come with nothing to offer Jesus except our need, but then we trust that He's done everything that we need to be made right with God. Jesus lived the perfect life for us; He died in our place; He rose again to give us new life. He is praying for us *right now* as our representative before God.

Everything's changed, but on the other hand, it still feels like your life is catching up. You still have questions and doubts.

Jesus spoke of a danger that we face at this stage. Some initially receive God's Word, but then "the cares of the world and the deceitfulness of riches and the desires for other things enter in and choke the word, and it proves unfruitful" (Mark 4:19). They don't stop believing, at least intellectually, but neither do they progress or grow. Other priorities take over. Sadly, we sometimes settle for intellectual assent and see following Jesus as a one-time decision rather than a whole-life journey in transformation that affects every part of our lives. Don't make this mistake. Don't settle for an individualistic, intellectual, complacent faith. It won't do you any good. You weren't meant to stay here.

Move to the next stage by learning the basics of the faith. Books like *Now That I'm a Christian* by Michael Patton or *The Walk* by Stephen Smallman can help you take your first steps toward growth.

If you haven't already begun to read the Bible and pray, then get started. Don't overcomplicate it. Find a study Bible in clear language and with helpful notes, and start reading a little every day. (I've listed some good ones in Appendix One.) Begin to tell God what's on your mind, and ask Him to help you.

But don't settle for just head knowledge. One of the best things that you can do to progress is to get involved with others who are a bit further along. Find a good church, and build relationships there. Ask questions. Learn from them. Tell them about your struggles. We're not meant to grow as believers on our own.

Make sure you avoid two dangers at this stage.

First, *don't settle for nominal belief.* If you consider yourself to be a believer, appreciate the Bible, and generally adhere to Christian values, but don't have an active, thriving relationship with God, you're missing out. Jesus is far too spectacular for us to follow Him like we'd follow a football team. We need to surrender to Him and follow Him with all of our broken, imperfect lives.

Second, *don't get stuck here.* You're not meant to stagnate at the Believing stage. Keep learning the basics, reading the Bible, praying, and learning from other Christians so that you can move to the next stage. Guard against comfort, complacency, apathy, unbelief, and self-sufficiency. Don't settle for anything but a whole-life pursuit of God that will begin to change every part of your life.

Stage Four: Growing

Believers are meant to grow. People at this stage begin to show that they have had a real encounter with God. They are conscious of experiencing God's grace. They know they're different than they used to be in how they think and act.

The Growing have declared their faith in Christ, and have joined a community of believers. They are learning the basics of Christianity and are wrestling with their questions and doubts.

This is a beautiful stage. In her book *The Secret Thoughts of an Unlikely Convert,* Rosaria Butterfield describes her experience moving into this stage:

> I started to obey God in my heart one step at a time. . . . I hoped that God would regard my obedience even in its double-mindedness. I started to go to the RP [Reformed Presbyterian] church fully, in my heart, for the whole purpose of worshiping God. I stopped caring if I looked like a freak there. I started to receive the friendship that the church members offered to me. I learned that we must obey in faith before we feel better or different. At this time, though, obeying in faith, to me, felt like throwing myself off a cliff. Faith that endures is heroic, not sentimental.[5]

In the Growing stage, everything has changed, and yet sometimes it feels like nothing's changed. It affects every area of life. It's messy, chaotic, full of questions, and glorious. It's an exciting stage, but we're also not meant to stay there.

The Growing stage is foundational for the rest of your journey. As you progress through the rest of the stages, you'll carry what you learn in this stage. *If you want to reach this stage and beyond, this book is written for you.* I want to help you develop the habits you need to grow and to make a difference in the lives of others.

Keep learning and applying the gospel. Develop habits that will help you to grow. (We'll cover these in coming chapters.) Start to help others grow too. Keep going!

Stage Five: Mentoring

Every Christian is meant to become a disciple-maker or mentor. Jesus Himself commanded us to make disciples (Matt. 28:18–20). Though we may continue to struggle with doubts and

sinful habits, individuals in this stage are growing in faith and repentance. They are active within their community of believers,
and are helping others to grow.

Sometimes the best we have to offer comes from our weak-
nesses, not our strengths. God allows us to come alongside others
who are going through difficulty. Because we've been there, or are
there, we're able to understand and help.

People in this stage pray for opportunities to pour into the lives
of others. They take seriously the advice given in Hebrews: "*Let
us consider* how to stir up one another to love and good works"
(Heb. 10:24). This is what sets them apart: not that they are experts, but that they're intentional in helping others grow.

This process of mentoring is ongoing, as we intentionally look
for ways to build up believers around us, spurring them on in their
spiritual growth journey. And the goal is to inspire them to go and
do the same (2 Tim. 2:2). We'll look at this more in chapter 9. Right
now, though, I want to encourage you to move here as quickly as
possible. You don't need to wait until you're further along. As long
as you're a step ahead of others, you're ready to move to this stage.

God isn't just calling you to become His follower. He's calling
you to mentor and disciple others. You can learn to do this, even
if you feel you have a long way to go. You are ahead of someone.
Your experience and wisdom can help them. You can spur someone else on and encourage them.

Stage Six: Maturing

There will never be a point in time when we finish growing,
at least in this life. Ironically, the more we grow, the more we're
aware of our sinfulness. Mature Christians, therefore, don't *feel*
spiritually mature. They increasingly grasp the magnitude of
God's holiness, their sinfulness, and the grace of the cross. Maturity and humility go together.

I'm thinking of two people I know who are at this stage. They seem free. I love being with them. They're far from perfect, but I feel different when I'm with them. They exude joy, and I feel encouraged whenever I see them. But I don't think they would even think of themselves as mature. That's what I love about them.

Maturing servants of Christ continue to discover deeper levels of repentance, and experience more of God's love and healing. They have varying levels of ability, but they lead to the measure of their giftedness (Matt. 25:14–30). They understand that "if there be degrees in glory, they will not be distributed according to our talents, but according to our faithfulness in using them."[6]

Mature Christians don't feel spiritually mature. They increasingly grasp the magnitude of God's holiness, their sinfulness, and the grace of the cross. Maturity and humility go together.

Maturing believers demonstrate faithfulness over a long period of time. They show "love, joy, peace, patience, kindness, goodness, faithfulness, gentleness, self-control" (Gal. 5:22–23). Often they have suffered deeply and have been broken. They want to help others live in the same freedom that they enjoy.

I can usually tell when I've met people at this stage. They're not usually impressed with themselves. They major in Jesus, and they're hungry for more freedom from guilt and sin. They want more newness of life, more power from the Holy Spirit. They always seem like safe people. Because they're aware of their sinfulness, they're not surprised by mine. Because they've been broken, they're not put off by others who suffer.

If you're at the Maturing stage, you may not even know it. Keep going. Be unimpressed with yourself but impressed with Christ. Allow your sufferings and your awareness of sin to draw you closer to Christ. Revel in the gospel. Continue to share your life with others, and trust that God will use you in your weakness.

MORE GROWTH, SAME WEEDS

I like thinking about growth using the Stages diagram. It helps us identify where we are right now, and what we need to do to move to the next stage. But our growth isn't always linear. We sometimes hit a wall—a time when old practices don't seem to help us like they used to, or we struggle with doubts and discouragement.

My friend Michael Thiessen, pastor of a church just north of Toronto, likes to compare our growth to that of a plant. No matter how much we grow, we often are surrounded by the same weeds, and maybe even some new ones.

I like this picture too. As we grow, it's possible that we may continue to face the same temptations and struggles. We'll outgrow some of them, but others will continue to plague us until God finishes His work within us. We'll conquer some temptations. Others will surround us even as we grow and mature. Don't get discouraged when you face the same old struggles. Keep growing.

KEEP GROWING

Recently I saw Elisabeth, a thirteen-month-old girl whose parents are part of our church. I remember learning that her mother was expecting. I remember the baby shower, and then hearing about Elisabeth's birth. I remember the first time her parents brought her to church. And I remember when she squealed throughout my sermon. It's hard to compete with someone who's so much cuter (and noisier) than me.

Whenever Elisabeth sees me now, she quickly turns her head. She's shy. I'm still the stranger she hardly knows. I love watching her, though. I love seeing her smile and giggle. I enjoy watching her toddle toward a toy and pick it up with delight. It's impossible not to delight in both her current stage and her continual growth.

Elisabeth will one day reach maturity. She's not meant to stay at her current stage. At the same time, there's a lot to celebrate and enjoy right now. Each stage is beautiful. Each stage builds on what's come before, and is a prelude to what's coming next.

This reminds me of the beauty and progression of spiritual growth. No matter what our current stage, God is at work. He creates curiosity among the Pre-Questioning; He takes the Questioning and woos them to Jesus; He transforms the Believing to the Growing. He then takes the Growing who think they have nothing to offer and leads them to Mentoring. Eventually, we become less impressed with ourselves and more impressed with Jesus and discover that we're Maturing. There's hope for each stage. We can celebrate our progress, help those who are behind us and with us, learn from those who are ahead of us, and take the next step. As long as we're alive, God invites us to grow and to take the next step.

CHAPTER SUMMARY

- Before we can grow, we must know where we are right now so we understand what's needed to take the next step.
- Growth isn't linear, but there are a series of stages on the path to spiritual maturity.
- The *Pre-Questioning* may not believe in God; they may believe in a different god. They aren't really interested in Jesus and His message. To move to the next stage, they need stimulating conversations, genuine friendships with Christians, and the opportunity to see the Christian faith lived out.
- The *Questioning* don't know much about Jesus, but are open. They can grow by learning the story of Christianity, exploring the Bible, and seeing the Christian faith lived out in community.
- The *Believing* identify as Christian. They can can grow by learning the basics of Christianity, reading the Bible, praying, and learning from other Christians.
- The *Growing* show evidence of a relationship with Jesus Christ, have joined a church community, and are learning the basics of the faith. They can grow by learning and applying the gospel, developing habits of grace, and helping others progress through the stages.
- The *Mentoring* are growing in faith and obedience, and helping others to grow. They can grow by looking for faithful people, entrusting the gospel to them, and helping them become disciple-makers.
- The *Maturing* don't often think much of themselves. They walk with a limp. They can continue to grow by sharing their lives with others, and by drawing close to Christ.

Questions for Personal Reflection or Group Discussion

1. What is your current stage?
2. What has worked well so far in your growth?
3. What steps should you be taking at your current stage?
4. Is there anything you have found especially helpful in your growth?
5. What can you do to encourage someone at an earlier stage?
6. What can you do to learn from someone who's ahead of you?

What Do I Do Now?

- Decide which stage describes where you are right now. Use the assessment at https://gospelforlife.com/stages.
- Pick one recommended action for someone at this stage, and begin to implement it.

CHAPTER FIVE

MASTER THE BASICS: KNOW, WORSHIP, OBEY

First master the fundamentals.

LARRY BIRD

Charlene was driving the car through snow-covered streets in Sudbury, four hours north of Toronto, when the dashboard lights started flashing. ABS! VSC! and some other mysterious lights signaled that something was wrong. She stopped, consulted the car manual, and kept driving. She didn't need to know all the details of what's wrong. She just needed to know that it was safe to drive, and that the mechanic could figure out what to do.

I love learning details of how complicated things (like cars) work. But sometimes I don't need to know all the details. I need to know that someone else knows, and that I can find out the information I need, but then I need to know what to do next. I just need to know about the basics.

Our growth is like that. I love studying theology and picking apart the intricacies of what happens as we grow. My goal in this chapter is to give you the basics: the three basics that form the basis of our growth as we apply the gospel to all of life. No matter how much we grow, we're always building on these basics.

Spiritual growth is complicated. But we can grow, without understanding all the intricacies of how growth happens, as we focus on the basics: *knowing, worshiping,* and *obeying* God. Everything else in this book will be about how to apply these three basics in our lives.

KNOW

New friends from South Africa just attended a baseball game. They're learning the rules of baseball. It's not much fun watching a sport that you don't understand.

In the same way, it's impossible to understand or enjoy life until we understand the most important things about life: who God is, what He's revealed about Himself, and how this world works. This knowledge is intellectual: it involves learning about God. But it's also deeply personal: it involves getting to know God in relationship.

> *We're not just learning a set of facts; we're getting to know God just like we get to know a person in relationship.*

We're not just learning a set of facts; we're getting to know God just like we get to know a person in relationship.

God is very concerned that we know *about* him. A. W. Tozer was right: "What comes into our minds when we think about God is the most important thing about us."[1] J. I. Packer goes even further in his classic book *Knowing God*:

> Knowing about God is crucially important for the
> living of our lives. As it would be cruel to an Amazo-
> nian tribesman to fly him to London, put him down
> without explanation in Trafalgar Square and leave
> him, as one who knew nothing of English or England,
> to fend for himself, so we are cruel to ourselves if we
> try to live in this world without knowing about the
> God whose world it is and who runs it. The world
> becomes a strange, mad, painful place, and life in it
> a disappointing and unpleasant business, for those
> who do not know about God. Disregard the study
> of God, and you sentence yourself to stumble and
> blunder through life blindfolded, as it were, with
> no sense of direction and no understanding of what
> surrounds you. This way you can waste your life and
> lose your soul.[2]

The Bible is clear about this priority as well. "Sanctify them in the truth; your word is truth," Jesus prayed (John 17:17). "I have stored up your word in my heart," wrote the psalmist, "that I might not sin against you" (Ps. 119:11).

So we must learn about God. We must get to know His nature: who He is, how He acts, and what He has done. This isn't important just for scholars, pastors, and intellectual types. In fact, we're all theologians. We all "do" theology everyday, making decisions based on what we believe is true. Joshua Harris writes, "Theology matters, because if we get it wrong, then our whole life will be wrong."[3]

We must also learn what He's taught us about how to live in this world. The Bible is full of practical advice on how to think and live. It teaches us about wisdom: the skill of living wisely in the world He's created. We do well to pay attention to what He's written. As we get to know God and the Bible, we learn what He wants from us in the practical details of our lives: in how we work, play, love, rest, and more. We learn what the Bible calls wisdom: the skill of living.

So how do we get to know Him? The best tool for building knowledge is to read, listen to, and study the Bible. This practice has a more significant impact on our overall growth than any other practice.[4] Sadly, studies show that many of us aren't reading the Bible regularly.[5] Using this tool is crucial for your growth.

> *We're all theologians. We all "do" theology everyday, making decisions based on what we believe is true.*

There are other ways, along with regular intake of Scripture, to learn more about God. Commit to regularly sit under the faithful preaching of the Word as it's explained and applied. Begin using a catechism to learn the major doctrines of Scripture.[6] Read an introductory theology book (see Appendix 1 for suggestions). Regularly read or listen to Christian books that teach and apply biblical truth. Listen to podcasts that teach and apply Scripture. Never before in history have we had so many resources to help us know God more.

"If we have no doctrine, we have no Christianity," says Fred Zaspel. "The deeper and clearer our understanding of Christian truth, the greater will be its sanctifying effect on us."[7] Knowing the truth is essential for growth.

WORSHIP

While it's essential to know God, it's not enough. We must also worship Him. To worship means to attribute worth and to hold Him as most valuable in our lives, of more value than anyone or anything else. It's the first of the Ten Commandments: "You shall have no other gods before me" (Ex. 20:3). Jesus reemphasized the importance of worship when He answered a question about the greatest commandment. "You shall love the Lord your God with all your heart and with all your soul and with all your mind," He said. "This is the great and first commandment" (Matt. 22:37–38).

We need to know about God, but we need to do more: we need to worship Him in His glory. Just as we're all theologians, we're also all worshipers: what we're beholding and what we value most is what we become.[8] Awe of God is a powerful thing.

To worship means to engage our hearts. We go beyond *knowing about* God to *knowing* Him. "I spend half my time telling Christians to study doctrine and the other half telling them that doctrine is not enough," quipped Martyn Lloyd-Jones.[9] Worship moves us from doctrine to devotion.

> *Just as we're all theologians, we're also all worshipers: what we're beholding and what we value most is what we become.*

One of my favorite hymns is "When I Survey the Wondrous Cross." The first verse leads us to behold the cross—to go beyond understanding it to really taking it in: "When I survey the wondrous cross / On which the Prince of glory died..." Isaac Watts helps us visualize Jesus' sacrificial death for us: sorrow and love flowing from His head, hands, and feet; the thorns on His head a rich crown. The author of the hymn doesn't get very far in beholding the cross before he describes some of the effects on his life:

- he counts his richest gain (his most valuable possession) as his loss;
- he pours contempt on his pride;

- he sacrifices the things that charm him most;
- he surrenders his soul, his life, his all.

Watts discovered a powerful tool for change: treasuring God's glory, especially through the lens of what Jesus has done for us. Become consumed with a vision of God and His beauty. Meditate on His holiness and His grace. Look at the cross. Consider what this means for your life now: you are accepted, you are delivered, you are not alone, and you have authority.[10] Keep beholding and it will surely change you.

It's what one old preacher called "the expulsive power of a new affection."[11] The only way to displace our misplaced affections is to replace them with something greater: with valuing and treasuring God. We change as we behold and cherish God's beauty and holiness. I think this is what Paul meant when he wrote:

> If then you have been raised with Christ, seek the
> things that are above, where Christ is, seated at the
> right hand of God. Set your minds on things that are
> above, not on things that are on earth. For you have
> died, and your life is hidden with Christ in God.
> When Christ who is your life appears, then you also
> will appear with him in glory. (Col. 3:1–4)

Paul encourages us to behold Christ and the things of God, and to set our minds on them. He goes further: he wants us to seek them and to pursue them. This pursuit begins to change our desires, and the change in our desires begins to change our behavior.

We all need to worship. Some of the best ways to do this include:

- *Go beyond reading and studying Scripture.* Meditate on it. Chew on it like a dog chews on a bone.
- *Engage in worship within a church.* Don't see worship as an

emotional experience, but as a way to immerse yourself in God's story and to rehearse the gospel to yourself again.

- *Grab hold of what God says to be true, and cling to it with your life.* I'm inspired by Jack Miller, a burned-out pastor and seminary professor who rediscovered God's missionary promises. It changed his life. "This marked a turning point in Jack's life and ministry. Not only did he go back to work with a renewed sense of purpose, he also had a new freedom to live and work only for God's glory."[12] Ask God for this in your own life.

OBEY

Knowing and worshiping God are powerful forces for change in our lives. In fact, growth is impossible without them. But they're incomplete without obedience. When we get to know God, and we learn to worship Him above everything and everyone else, we can then grow in obedience.

Obedience involves two activities: turning away from sin, and engaging in activities that help us grow.

Negatively, *we obey by avoiding sin.* The Bible repeatedly gives us a list of sins to avoid: things like "sexual immorality, impurity, sensuality, idolatry, sorcery, enmity, strife, jealousy, fits of anger, rivalries, dissensions, divisions, envy, drunkenness, orgies, and things like these" (Gal. 5:19–21). The assumption is that we can avoid them. Now that God lives within us, He gives us the ability to see sin for what it is and to avoid it. We don't always succeed, but we can learn to avoid sin more as we depend on God. Sin no longer has any mastery over us (Rom. 6:14). We still feel its influence, and we're tempted by it, but it no longer controls us like it used to. Our job is to do what God is already doing within us: kill sin. As John Owen writes, this is now our daily work:

> Do you mortify;
> do you make it your daily work;
> be always at it while you live;
> cease not a day from this work;
> be killing sin or it will be killing you.[13]

Positively, *we obey God by keeping His commands.* Jesus connects obedience to love: "If you love me, you will keep my commandments" (John 14:15). Before, we were powerless to obey. Once God begins to change us, we not only want to obey God out of love, but we're *able* to do so. As we read commands in the Bible, we will increasingly find that we're able to obey where once we struggled—not only because we know and love God more, but because He's at work within us, giving us the power to obey.

Here are some ways to grow in obedience:

- Search in Scripture for the clear commands that He's given you to obey.
- Remind yourself that, despite appearances, sin no longer has power over you (Rom. 6:14). Through Christ, you have the power to obey.
- When you sin, confess your sins to God (1 John 1:9).

DO IT TOGETHER

Know God, worship Him, and obey. We never advance beyond these essentials. We'll explore practices that allow us to master these basics in the rest of the book, but not before I leave you with a key for mastering these basics that we're likely to miss.

I have a blind spot, and you do too. When I read the Bible, I tend to read it as if "you" refers to "me." "*You* are the salt of the earth," Jesus says (Matt. 5:13), and I think He's talking about me, or at least each individual who follows Him. "Put on the whole armor of God, that *you* may be able to stand against the schemes of the devil" (Eph. 6:11), and I picture myself standing alone with God's armor ready to take a stand.

What we miss so often is that the Bible isn't written to solitary individuals but to the church. More often than not we could read "y'all" rather than you.

What we miss so often is that the Bible isn't written to solitary individuals but to the church. More often than not we could read "y'all" rather than "you." The Christian life doesn't make sense when lived alone. We were meant to live it in community with others.

We need others to grow, and Scripture reflects that with admonitions to love one another, honor one another, accept one another, serve one another, carry one another's burdens, be kind and compassionate to one another, submit to one another, admonish one another, encourage each other, confess our sins to one another, and more.[14]

An African proverb says, "If you want to go quickly, go alone. If you want to go far, go together." We can try to grow spiritually by ourselves, unencumbered by the quirks and demands of others. But if we want to go far in our growth, we must grow in community. Biblical community is one of God's most powerful tools for growth.

Here are some ways that we can pursue community:

- When reading Scripture, default to reading the collective "y'all" rather than the individual "you."
- Look for ways to practice the "one another" commands of Scripture. Lean into activities that allow you to form deeper relationships with other Christians.

- Lean into the mess. When community gets messy, frustrating, and ugly, it's usually a good sign, not a bad one. Stick with it. People are messy, including us.
- Integrate community as a regular part of your life. Look for activities you can do with others: eating together, shopping together, working together, and more. Create rhythms of relationship.

No matter how complicated things get, we can always return to these basics. The Christian life involves knowing God better, worshiping and loving Him more, and growing in our obedience. As we work on these basics in community, we will experience change.

Let's look, then, at the habits and practices that will allow us to master these basics.

CHAPTER SUMMARY

- Spiritual growth involves mastering the basics: knowing, worshiping, and obeying God.
- Knowing God involves learning about Him and knowing Him relationally. Knowing God helps us know how to live well.
- Worshiping God involves learning to love and value Him above everything and everyone else.
- Obeying God involves avoiding sin and obeying His commands.
- We grow best in community.

Questions for Personal Reflection or Group Discussion

1. What practical steps can you take to get to know God better?
2. What practices help you to value God above everything and everyone else?
3. How does knowing God better and worshiping Him more help with obedience?
4. Why do you think it's so important that we grow in community?

What Do I Do Now?

- Spend some time thinking about who God is and what He's done for you, and thank Him for it.
- Pick an area in which you want to grow in your obedience, and ask God for His help.
- Share something that encourages you about your growth with another Christian.

CHAPTER SIX

HOW HABITS
HELP YOU GROW

Champions don't do extraordinary things.
They do ordinary things, but they do them
without thinking, too fast for the other team to react.
They follow the habits they've learned.

TONY DUNGY

We all want to change. It's just a lot harder than we thought.

We now spend 10 billion dollars on self-improvement in the United States alone.[1] Books, seminars, and coaching programs promise real change. You can learn to be happier, smarter, sexier, more successful, and more popular. We know what to do, or at least can buy a book about it. If we need the extra help, experts are happy to help us (for a small fee, of course). But we still struggle to change.

We even find it hard to change when our lives are at stake. If a well-informed, trusted authority figure told you that you had to make a difficult and enduring change in the way that you think and act, you likely think that you'd comply. In reality, most don't. The scientifically studied odds are nine to one against you changing, even when your life's at stake.[2] That's grim news for those who want to change.

You would think it's easier for those of us who are followers of Jesus. In some ways it is. When we believe, the Holy Spirit indwells us and begins to change us from the inside out. He also gives us a new heart. God is so committed to completing the job that He guarantees the work will get done (Rom. 8:29–30; Phil. 1:6). The end result will be impressive.

In the meantime, though, we look more like fixer-uppers in the middle of a massive construction project. We're aware of our flaws and tripped up by our tendencies. We can relate to the apostle Paul's words: "The desire to do what is good is with me, but there is no ability to do it. For I do not do the good that I want to do, but I practice the evil that I do not want to do" (Rom. 7:18–19 CSB).

Growth is possible, and God promises He will change us. But we're often frustrated because we're not changing as quickly or as much as we'd like. Is it possible we've been going about it in the wrong way?

WRONG WAYS TO CHANGE

When we want to change, we typically try one or more of the following approaches:

New information—We read books, watch videos, listen to sermons, and attend Bible studies. We think that new information will change us. When this doesn't work, we go looking for even more information. We become more knowledgeable, but we often don't change. We become educated beyond the level of our obedience.

Big goals—We also set big goals to start or stop behaviors. We want to read the Bible every year, but then get stuck in Leviticus. We want to stop surfing social media, but find ourselves scrolling through once again in a moment of boredom, avoidance, or procrastination. Most of us have set big goals to make big changes, but have failed to see the transformation we desired. "Your audacious life goals are fabulous. We're proud of you for having them," writes Seth Godin. "But it's possible that those goals are designed to distract you from the thing that's really frightening you—the shift in daily habits that would mean a re-invention of how you see yourself."[3]

Willpower—We think we need more willpower, but find it doesn't last as long as we'd like. Some argue that willpower is quickly depleted. Others argue that we can learn to increase our willpower, and boost it when it's weak. Either way, willpower can help us, but it can't create the consistent, sustainable change we want in our lives.

I'm shocked by how often I've relied on these when trying to change myself, or to help others grow. In particular, I *love* new information. I'm always tempted to look for the next book that will give me the information that I need. This tendency reflects an incomplete or deficient view of my own humanity. We're more than a sum of our knowledge, goals, and willpower. If we keep trying these approaches, we'll keep failing in our efforts to change.

It's time to try to new approach. Surprisingly, change involves leveraging something we already use every single day of our lives, often without noticing it.

Living by Habit

We live by habit. We're not even aware of it, but we do. All of us—the overwhelmed, imperfect, structured, spontaneous, rigid, and flexible—are already expert habit-keepers. The issue isn't whether habits will work for us or not. They already do.

Scientists estimate that about 40 percent of our activities are performed each day in almost the same situations.[4] In other words, almost half of our lives are run by habit. Habits aren't just for disciplined people. We *all* operate by habit. We all look for behaviors that work, and then begin to repeat those actions. Habits help free up our attention from routine tasks so we don't have to rethink the same decisions every day.

A habit, according to the Oxford Dictionary, is "a settled or regular tendency or practice, especially one that is hard to give up."[5] A habit is a behavior that's become automatic, comfortable, and part of how we think and operate.

As I write this at 10:30 in the morning, I realize that my morning has been driven by my habits:

- I woke up on the same side of the bed as usual around the same time as usual.
- I spent the first hour alone in the kitchen reading my Bible, praying, and journaling.
- I prepared breakfast at 7:00, and sat in the same seat as I usually do at the breakfast table. My son and my wife did the same.
- I brushed my teeth in the same pattern. I developed this pattern after I found myself daydreaming while brushing, and forgetting what teeth I'd already cleaned.
- I left for the same coffee shop, ordered an Americano and Hobbit muffin, and sat in my regular seat. The staff knew what I was going to order before I ordered it.

In my family, each of us has a different set of habits, but our mornings unfolded in the same way as they usually do. When we don't follow our habits, we feel a little discombobulated. (My son, who is usually punctual, slept in today and didn't like it.)

Unfortunately, I also have bad habits. I check my phone too often. I'm sometimes too addicted to checking email and social media when I should be focused on something else. My wife Charlene could fill a couple of pages with all of my bad habits. Most of the time, I'm not even aware I'm doing them.

For better or worse, we live according to habit. We think we live our lives according to design or thought, when almost half of our lives operates on autopilot.

To change, we need to learn how to create habits that help us become the person we want to be. We need habits that put us in the path of God's grace.

HABITS AND SPIRITUAL GROWTH

One of the most insightful thinkers on the role of habits in the spiritual life is James K. A. Smith, author of *You Are What You Love*. Smith explains our misperception that we're thinking beings or "brains-on-a-stick." We expect we can think our way to growth. Smith argues that we're lovers more than thinkers. In the end, we're driven by what we love and desire more than by what we think.

How, then, do we shape our desires? Smith argues that we'll only change our desires by changing our habits. Good, godly habits become woven into our character so that we begin to desire the right things. "To become virtuous is to internalize the law (and the good to which the law points) so that you follow it more or less automatically," he writes.[6] It becomes "second nature"—which implies that our first nature isn't what it's meant to be. In other words, we don't change through thinking. We change by changing what we love, and we change what we love through habits.

Experience shows this to be true. The people I know who tower over me in their spiritual lives are people who love God from the heart. The reason they love God from the heart is because they've followed habits for years that have shaped their desires. Their second nature has become first nature, and it puts them in the paths of grace because of the habits that they follow. They can't imagine living otherwise.

I think of one person I've grown to respect. She's godly and one of the most spiritually mature people I've met. I think I know how she got there. "Reading God's Word is not difficult for me," she writes. "I almost can't start my day unless I've had my Bible reading time."[7] She is honest about her struggles, and yet I see consistent growth in her life because she's built habits that help her grow closer to God.

Habits are formative. Rather than waking up every day and deciding anew whether we will take in God's Word, pray about our days, or live in community, we can make those decisions once and incorporate these habits into our daily life. This then makes the behaviors automatic. This will help to keep our wandering hearts on track with the means that God has given us to live in His grace. We need "habitual obedience."[8]

In the end, we're driven by what we love and desire more than by what we think.

Habits also help to shift the focus from the activity to the person of Jesus. When we begin a new behavior, it takes a lot of mental energy. When we first learn to read the Bible or pray, we have to think about every step we take. The focus at first isn't on the Word or on God: it's on our methods. When our obedience becomes habitual, we're able to direct our focus past the activities themselves to the One we're pursuing. The power of a spiritual discipline isn't in the discipline itself, after all. The disciplines exist to bring us to Jesus and to put us in the path of His grace.

"Your habits are, in fact, one of the most important things

about you," writes David Mathis. "Those repeated actions you take over and over, almost mindlessly, reveal your true self over time as much as anything else."[9]

Hacking Habits

Our lives are shaped by what we do, and what we do most regularly happens out of habit. The key to change, then, is to change our habits.

The good news is that once we've built good habits, they're relatively easy to maintain. We don't have to decide what to do every day. We'll just do them. I never have to decide what side of the bed to sleep on. I decided that long ago, and now I never give it a thought.

The bad news is that habits are hard to start, and they're hard to end. Ask anyone who's tried to quit smoking or wake up earlier in the morning. Habits are powerful, and good habits have the power to change how we live. Because good habits are so powerful, they can be hard to work with.

You may have heard that it takes twenty-one days to form a habit. That would be nice if it were true. We could change our lives in just three weeks. According to a study published in the *European Journal of Social Psychology*, it actually takes an average of two months (sixty-six days) for a new behavior to become automatic. The actual time depends on a number of factors, including the behavior, person, and circumstances. It can take anywhere from 18 to 254 days for people to form a new habit.[10]

We not only need to learn how to form new habits; we need to learn how to break habits too. If we are going to grow in our lives, we need to learn how to hack our habits.

So let's get practical and start hacking habits.

SEVEN BEST PRACTICES FOR BUILDING HABITS

1. Start small.

One of the best (and free) programs I've ever taken is Tiny Habits, a five-day habit-building program created by Stanford behaviorist BJ Fogg.[11] Most of us try to change by creating an epiphany, which is very hard to do, or by making sweeping changes in our lives. Fogg argues that it's better to change our environment to support the changes we'd like to make, and then to take baby steps. Make it so easy that you can't fail.

Want to floss your teeth? Don't set a goal to floss your teeth every night. You'll probably fail. Commit to flossing one tooth, and trigger that behavior by something else that you already do. Chances are that you'll be able to keep that commitment, and that you won't stop with that one tooth (although you can if you want).

When you want to make a change, don't start with a big action. Start with one action that's so small that you can't fail. If you try it and still don't succeed, shrink it even more. Choose something that takes such minimal effort that you don't need to rely on willpower to make it happen. Don't try to build multiple habits at the same time. Focus on one.

The goal at the beginning isn't even to create the change we want. It's to build the foundation for habits. It's to build up the level of performance we want when the behavior becomes automatic.

Shrink the challenge. Pick a behavior, shrink it, and then shrink it again until you're 80 percent sure that you can practice that behavior consistently. Don't start by setting a goal to read ten chapters of the Bible every day; start by committing to read the Bible for a minute each day. Don't resolve to pray for an hour every day; begin with praying for thirty seconds each morning, and build from there.

2. Shape the environment

Going to the gym used to be a hassle. I'd have to get in my car and drive fifteen minutes. Now that we live in a condo, the gym is less than a minute away. Going to the gym still requires effort, but the environment makes it more likely.

Environment shapes behavior. A fridge full of veggies will shape our behavior, and so will a cupboard full of chips. Spend some time thinking about an environment that will help you create the habits you want to build. To build the habit of reading the Bible in the morning, find a good Bible and leave it out before you go to bed. To develop the habit of praying before checking social media, delete the app(s) from your phone. Shape your environment so it supports the habits you want to create.

3. Use triggers and rewards.

According to BJ Fogg, we can build habits by following a few basic steps:

- **Get specific**—pick the desired behavior
- **Make it easy**—simplify the behavior so it's easy to do
- **Trigger the behavior**—use a trigger to prompt the action, which leads to a reward[12]

It's not enough to decide on our desired outcome and the behaviors we want to practice. We also need to focus on the triggers and rewards.

When building habits, then, it helps to set up some good triggers:

- Is there a set time to practice your new habit? Sometimes it helps to have a set time every day to perform a set of actions so that they become automatic.
- Is there a set place? Sitting in a particular spot every day,

for instance, can signal that it's time to start a particular set of actions.

- Is there a reminder or preceding event? For instance, my phone buzzes me every day at 10:02 a.m., signaling me that it's time to pray for more workers for the harvest (Luke 10:2). Link a new habit to an existing routine or habit.
- Are there other people who can encourage me? I'm part of a Bible reading group this year. Emails from other group participants help remind me to practice my Bible-reading habit.

Rewards are also a powerful way to build habits. The reward doesn't have to be elaborate. Look for rewards that are inherent in the habit. For instance, I find that coffee and prayer with Charlene every morning leads to its own reward: a happier marriage. Celebration also serves as an effective reward, so notice and celebrate your progress.

4. Focus on making progress.

One of the reasons we quit is that we notice the gap between where we are now and where we'd like to be. We have an image of perfection, and we get frustrated that we are nowhere close.

I noticed this when Charlene and I started a nutrition program. I found it intimidating to get started, especially when we had so far to go.

But the nutrition program taught us one simple habit every two weeks. We weren't supposed to even think about other habits. We were just supposed to follow the assigned habit for those two weeks. Over the course of a year they gave us twenty-six simple but profound habits. Together, they stacked to create significant changes in our lives. We're still practicing most of those habits today, mostly without thinking about them.

We never would have made such sweeping changes if we had tried to make them all at once. The program taught us to focus on making progress—

> *Taking small actions consistently matters more than taking big actions occasionally.*

often small progress—rather than focusing on our desired outcome. They regularly reminded us to *pursue progress, not perfection.*

Small habits, done consistently and stacked together, create massive change. Pick a small habit, so small that you can do it consistently. When you've got that small habit down, add another one. Stack a few of these small habits together and you'll start to see some big changes in your life. Taking small actions consistently matters more than taking big actions occasionally. Look back at how far you've come and celebrate your progress.

5. Keep going, even when you fail.

Many of us tend to be all-or-nothing. When we succeed, we keep going. When we fail, we give up. If we apply this approach to habits, we'll be doomed before we start.

We're not building habits in a lab environment. We're building habits in the middle of normal, complicated lives full of work deadlines, dishes, difficult relationships, car accidents, and baby vomit. We're also not machines. We're inconsistent and imperfect, and even consistent people are inconsistent sometimes.

When you're building a habit and you fail, just pick yourself up and keep going. Practice a clean-slate policy. The gospel is big enough to handle our failures. Keep going.

6. Know yourself.

To succeed with habits, I need a structure to follow. My wife, though, needs more than structure. She also needs social support.

A few years ago, we started a couple of habit-based programs together. I assumed that I'd do well, because I generally thrive with structured programs. To my surprise, Charlene surpassed me in both consistency and results. It was the perfect program for both of us: I got the structure I needed, and because we worked through the programs together, Charlene got the social support she needed. I had concluded she wasn't good at habits. I was wrong. We just needed different things to succeed.

I'm convinced that everyone can build habits, but that we may need different approaches to succeed. Some of us just need a structured approach. Others need to tackle habits with others through external accountability or social support. Some need an approach that's stimulating and that offers variety. We're all different, but we can leverage our differences to find an approach that works for us.

The key is to think about what's worked for you in the past, and to keep experimenting until you find an approach to habits that works for you.

- If you need lots of stimulation and variety, experiment with approaches to habits that stimulate you. Gamify your habits. Do them with others. Build variety into your plan.
- If you like to complete checkboxes, then leverage the value of structure.
- If you need external accountability or social support, then find others who can support you as you build habits. Don't try to build them alone.

Think about what's worked for you in the past, and do more of that. Keep experimenting. Look for others who are like you, and find out how they've learned to build habits.

7. Pay attention to resistance.

The above six practices usually work. When we start small, shape the environment, tie habits to existing behaviors and rewards, focus on progress rather than perfection, and practice a clean-slate policy, habits become a lot easier. Most of the time, habits flounder because we're too ambitious, don't set triggers, and give up when we're not perfect. It also helps to know ourselves so that we can structure habits around our tendencies.

But sometimes, even when we engage all six practices, we still find ourselves stuck. When this happens, go back and make the habit even smaller, and review the other best practices. But if you're still stuck, it's time to pay attention to resistance.

Resistance is the part of us that works against the change that we'd like. Resistance can come from ambivalence, competing values, or the fear of change.

Right now, for instance, I'm having a hard time getting up in the morning. I love mornings, so it's surprising to me that I'm resisting my normal morning routine. As I think about it, though, I realize that I usually have less energy this time of year. It's cold and dark in the morning. I'm responding by trying to get extra rest and by simplifying my morning routine so that it's more manageable. If I didn't pay attention and make adjustments, the cycle of resistance would continue, and I'd probably end up staying in bed and missing my morning routine altogether.

Resistance is often a clue that we need to make adjustments so that our habits work better for us. When we don't pay attention, we miss out on making these adjustments, and we can end up in danger of sabotaging the habits we're trying to create.

Here are some steps that you can take when you notice resistance:

- *Notice it and name what's going on.* This is a big step in itself. Explore why you may be resisting this new habit. Gently uncover why you might be resisting change.
- *Revisit your motivation.* Why do you want to build this new habit? Clarifying the "why" behind a new habit can be motivating. If you're not clear on why you want to build the new habit, keep working until you get clarity. If you can't find clarity, consider changing the habit.
- *If you feel ambivalent, dig deeper.* Ask two crazy questions: What's bad about this new habit? What's good about *not* doing this new habit? Uncover competing priorities and values, and try to work around them if you can. You may be resisting getting up early to read the Bible, for instance, because you don't want to lose too much sleep. Look for a way to read the Bible that doesn't cause you to lose sleep.
- *Bring your fears to God.* Fear can cause us to resist building new habits. I've found it helpful to confess my fears to God, and then identify what might be lurking underneath those fears. Our fears reveal the things that we're trying to protect. Fear can be a God-given gift: we fear things that could cause us harm, like walking too close to a cliff. But fears can also reveal issues in our lives that need repentance: we fear embarrassing ourselves, for instance, because we get our identity from what other people think about us. Confess your fears to God, and ask for His help in dealing with them.

If you get stuck in building a new habit, and you're practicing the first six principles, it's usually a sign that you're encountering resistance. The first six practices take work, but they're pretty simple. Overcoming our resistance can take a bit more work, and may even involve uncovering some damaging behaviors in our lives.

Start small, use triggers and rewards, focus on progress, and keep going even when you fail. Learn how to adjust your habits for yourself. Notice any resistance. Explore it, pray about it, and ask for help from others.

Practicing these principles doesn't look like much, but the more you use them to create small habits, the more they'll combine to create big changes in your life.

HABITS AREN'T THE POINT

I'm a big believer in habits. Because so much of our lives are run on autopilot, it's impossible to change without changing our habits. Our habits form us into the people that we are. I've never seen anyone change without them.

Habits are a great way to build discipline into our lives, especially for those of us who aren't disciplined. Donald Whitney, who's written a lot about spiritual disciplines, comments, "I've never known a man or woman who came to spiritual maturity except through discipline."[13] The apostle Paul commanded, "Train yourself for godliness" (1 Tim. 4:7). Habits help us so that we're disciplined in doing the things we need to do, even when we don't feel like it, and even when we don't think of ourselves as disciplined people.

I've never met anyone godly who hasn't developed habits that support their growth.

Habits are essential, but in the end, they aren't the point. If we focus on the habits and disciplines themselves, we'll become arrogant and judgmental of others who aren't as successful, or we'll become discouraged when we fail. It's possible to build great habits and completely miss the point, which is ongoing spiritual growth and intimacy with God.[14] D. A. Carson reminds us, "The truly transformative element is not the discipline itself, but the worthiness of the task undertaken: the value of prayer, the value of reading God's Word."[15]

The point, in the end, is our pursuit of God. We need habits that support that pursuit. We won't pursue God without them. They are ways of putting ourselves in the path of God's grace. David Mathis compares the habits to flipping the light switch: we don't produce the electricity any more than we control the supply of God's grace. But there are ways of turning on that power in our lives. The habits allow us to access God's grace so that it flows into our lives. "There are paths along which he has promised his favor," he writes.[16]

> *It's possible to build great habits and completely miss the point, which is ongoing spiritual growth and intimacy with God.*

Let's build habits that put us in the path of God's grace. Start small, pursue progress, and wipe the slate clean when you fail. Gradually add other habits until your life is increasingly shaped by the good behaviors that have become second nature to you.

But as you build your habits, remember that the habits are essential, but that they're not the point. They're means to an end, and that end is God. Build habits that remind you it's God who you need in the end. He promises, after all, to reward those who seek Him (Heb. 11:6). Let's build lives with habits that support the activities that God promises to bless.

CHAPTER SUMMARY

- We don't change by acquiring new information, setting big goals, or relying on willpower.

- We live almost half of our lives by habits. Our habits shape us. To grow, we must change our habits.
- To build a habit, start small. Make the new habit so small that you're at least 80 percent confident that you'll be able to practice the habit consistently. Keep shrinking the habit until it's too easy.
- Use triggers (time, place, preceding events, accountability) to help you build a new habit. Enjoy the inherent reward when you succeed.
- Focus on progress, not perfection.
- Practice a clean-slate policy.
- Know your style when it comes to building habits, and frame your choices based on the approach that works best for you.
- When you find yourself resisting a new habit, look for ambivalence, competing values, or fear of change. Pray about your resistance, and ask for help from others.
- Habits aren't the point. Habits are a means of pursuing God.

Questions for Personal Reflection or Group Discussion

1. Why do you think so many people have a hard time changing, even when the stakes are high?
2. This chapter argues that new knowledge, goals, and willpower aren't enough. Do you agree? Which of these approaches have you tried in your life?
3. When have you successfully built a new habit in your life? What was the new habit? What can you learn from your experience?
4. Which of the seven best practices do you enjoy the most? Which do you find hardest?

What Do I Do Now?

- Pick a habit that you've been trying to develop, and shrink it so it's so small that you can't fail.
- Think of a time that you've successfully built a new habit. Try to identify the factors that helped you succeed in building that habit. Write down 2–3 lessons that you can repeat as you try to develop new habits in the future.

CHAPTER SEVEN

THREE CORE HABITS WE NEVER OUTGROW

Nearly every area of life can be boiled down to some core task, some essential component, that must be mastered if you truly want to be good at it.

JAMES CLEAR

One of my friends is a former paramedic. When he began his training, the instructor told him that he would teach only three things: the basics of airway, breathing, and circulation, or the ABCs. "The physician told us he could teach a monkey how to be a paramedic in a week," he says. Understandably, the students felt insulted. They'd just spent years studying to qualify for the program, and had paid thousands of dollars in tuition. Surely there's more to being a paramedic, they argued.

The instructor agreed, sort of. There was more to learn—not more topics, but more about each of the ABCs. They would go deeper into the basics, but they'd never move beyond them. "All it takes is the basic skills," my friend says. "But, he said, it would take years for us to learn how to apply them."

This principle applies to every area of life, including our spiritual growth. The way to grow is to master the basics—a job that takes a lifetime. To grow spiritually, focus on three core habits. We never outgrow these habits, so keep coming back to them.

WE NEVER MOVE BEYOND THE BASICS

In July 1961, thirty-eight members of the Green Bay Packers football team gathered for the first day of training camp. The previous season ended when the Packers squandered a lead late in the game and lost the NFL Championship to the Philadelphia Eagles.

Their coach, Vince Lombardi, addressed the group of professional athletes. Months earlier, they'd come within minutes of winning the biggest prize in their sport. Lombardi stood in the group, raised a football, and said, "Gentlemen, this is a football." He started at the beginning and covered the fundamentals of the playbook starting from page one. At one point, Max McGee, the Packers' Pro Bowl wide receiver, joked, "Uh, Coach, could you slow down a little? You're going too fast for us."[1] Lombardi smiled, but continued with the basics. Six months later, the Packers defeated the New York Giants 37–0 to win the NFL Championship.

Every follower of Jesus needs to master the core gospel habits that will keep them growing for a lifetime. We never move beyond them. I've noticed that some complain that the core habits are too basic. Usually, when I press them, I discover that they don't practice them consistently. They would like to move on to something more advanced without mastering—or being mastered by—the basics. I've also noticed that when I talk to more mature believers about the core habits, their eyes light up. They feel like they're just getting started with the basics.

No matter how much we grow, we'll never grow beyond building three basic gospel habits: reading or listening to the Bible, praying, and pursuing worship and fellowship within a church community.

Core Habit One: Reading or Listening to the Bible

Reading or listening to absorb the Bible is crucial for spiritual growth. Donald Whitney, a leading teacher on spiritual disciplines, writes, "No spiritual discipline is more important than the intake of God's Word. Nothing can substitute for it. There simply is no healthy Christian life apart from a diet of the milk and meat of Scripture."[2]

The late philanthropist and pastor George Müller said something similar: "The vigour of our spiritual life will be in exact proportion to the place held by the Bible in our life and thoughts."[3] Jesus Himself affirmed the importance of the Bible when He quoted a passage from the Hebrew Scriptures: "Man does not live by bread alone, but man lives by every word that comes from the mouth of the LORD" (Deut. 8:3; cf. Matt. 4:4). Every spiritually mature person I've known has made the regular intake of God's Word a priority in their life.

Despite the importance of reading or listening to the Bible, most of us haven't developed this habit. A study in Canada found that self-identified Christians did not read or engage with the Bible much more than Canadians in general. Only one in five Christians reflect on the meaning of the Bible for their lives a few times a week.[4] "We are not reading the Bible, much less reading it well," comments George Guthrie, a professor of New Testament.

Ask one hundred church members if they have read the Bible today, and eighty-four of them will say no. Ask them if they have read the Bible at least once in the past week, and sixty-eight of them will say no. Even more disconcerting, ask those one hundred church members if reading or studying the Bible has made any significant difference in the way they live their lives. Only thirty-seven out of one hundred will say yes.[5]

The solution isn't a guilt trip. The solution is to build a habit of reading or listening to the Bible using the best practices for building habits.

Fortunately, we live in a golden age of resources for Bible reading. Videos, study Bibles, Bible reading plans, and books on how to study the Bible give us everything we need to get started. Still, many of us are intimidated, especially if we've gotten stuck in the past or never read the Bible on our own.

Here are some tips on building the habit of reading Scripture:

Find the why. Reading or listening to the Bible takes some effort. You will probably get stuck. You'll run into some parts of the Bible that are difficult to understand or that frustrate you. Spend some time reflecting on the importance of Scripture—even the hard parts! Clarify for yourself why reading or listening to Scripture is important. And remember that we can't follow God if we don't know who He is or what He desires. Reading Scripture is essential for growth. Remind yourself often. Keep coming back to these reasons.

Start small. Pick a goal that's realistic. It's better to read for five minutes a day consistently rather than fifteen minutes a day sporadically. Shrink the habit until you're confident you'll be able to practice it consistently at least 80 percent of the time.

Pick a format. Pick a good Bible version that's both accurate and understandable. (See Appendix 1 for recommended resources). If you want to read, pick a good study Bible, or if you'd like to try something different, pick up a reader's Bible that omits the chapters and verses. You may also want to consider picking an audio Bible, particularly if you don't enjoy reading or if you've found yourself bogged down in the past. Bryce Hales, a pastor who participated in Gospel for Life Discipleship, switched from reading to listening to the Bible every day and found that it was helpful. "Every morning I go for a walk, listening to the Bible and then spending time in prayer. It's a really simple change, but it's made a big difference in my life."

Use tools. Good tools make a big difference. A study Bible helps you understand the overall themes of Bible, the big picture of each book within the Bible, and the details of each passage. The free videos produced by The Bible Project[6] can help transform the way we see and understand challenging parts of Scripture. I have a friend who used their video on Leviticus (one of the more challenging books for many of us) in his sermon, and received a standing ovation. Use some of the great tools in Appendix 1 to help you understand and go deeper as you read and listen.

Read or listen with others. Some of us prefer to be alone. Others of us do much better as part of a group when tackling a project, and will do better when we read or listen to Scripture with others. Find some friends who want to work through the Bible, and set a goal to follow the same plan. Create a Facebook group, text thread, or email list and invite others to join you. Accountability and support from others can help to keep us on track.

Reading and listening to God's Word helps to shape our hearts. It helps us see the world differently, and to become accustomed to God's ways. And yet, it's hard. Many people struggle to develop this habit even though they understand its importance.

"Nobody ever outgrows Scripture," said the British preacher Charles Spurgeon. "The book widens and deepens with our years."[7] Keep reading, listening, and memorizing Scripture. Meditate on it. There's no other habit that will change you as much as this one.

Core Habit Two: Prayer

The strange thing about prayer is that it's easy and hard at the same time. It's easy: anyone can do it. Nobody needs to learn how. The smallest child can do it. People who don't even believe in God feel compelled to pray. It's almost like we can't help ourselves. Jared Wilson defines prayer as "acknowledged helplessness—spilling our guts."[8] Spilling our guts shouldn't be that hard.

The strange thing, though, is that it is. I don't know anyone who feels accomplished in prayer. A publisher once approached Sinclair Ferguson, an esteemed Scottish theologian, and asked him to write a book about prayer. He felt flattered but demurred. The author of such a book would, he said, need to be older, more seasoned, and more prayerful. He even suggested some names.

The editor smiled. He had already asked the well-seasoned Christian leaders that Ferguson had mentioned. They, too, had declined for the same reasons.

"Wise men," Ferguson says. "Who can write or speak at any length easily on the mystery of prayer?"[9]

We're all beginners when it comes to prayer. This is good news, though, because it puts us in the right place to learn how to pray. The secret to prayer is helplessness. Paul Miller writes, "Prayer is bringing your helplessness to Jesus. . . . The very thing we are allergic to—our helplessness—is what makes prayer work. It works because we *are* helpless. We can't do life on our own."[10]

I'm learning that prayer is about coming to God with our helplessness and the mess of our lives. It means telling God exactly what's on our minds and asking for His help. I want to come to God all put together; God wants me to come to Him as I am. Jesus died for the real you, so come to God with the real you. Come with your temptations, struggles, doubts, and anxieties. Come confessing that you don't want to pray. Come as you are.

Jesus died for the real you, so come to God with the real you. Come with your temptations, struggles, doubts, and anxieties.

After all, God invites us to come. I wake up regularly and look over at my wife with amazement. She *wants* to be in relationship with me. She knows the worst about me, and yet she's still here. It is amazing that Charlene loves me this much and wants to spend her life with me. How much more amazing is it that God wants a relationship with us and longs to hear from us. As a father delights in his children coming to him, so God delights in our approach, even if we come full of need and not as together as we'd like.

Our mistake is that we tend to see prayer as a duty rather than a delight. We should approach God not because we *have* to, but because we *get to*. He loves us. He cares for us. He invites us into relationship with Him. God actually wants to hear what's on our minds.

I've found three practices helpful when it comes to prayer.

First, see prayer as a way to manage your life. I got this idea from Paul Miller.

> Prayer is where I do my best work as a husband, dad, worker, and friend. . . . I'm actually managing my life through my daily prayer time. I'm shaping my heart, my work, my family—in fact, everything that is dear to me—through prayer in fellowship with my heavenly Father. I'm doing that because I don't have

control over my heart and life or the hearts and lives of those around me. But God does.[11]

Charlene and I found this a few years ago when we felt overwhelmed. Charlene was changing careers. We were starting a new ministry together. I was juggling ministry pressures. On top of this, we'd received some devastating news that hit us emotionally. Charlene and I had always struggled to pray together. Suddenly, out of desperation, it was our only choice. We began to pray together in the morning, and I also learned to pray throughout the day whenever I felt overwhelmed, which was a lot. I wish I hadn't waited so long to learn this. Rather than trying to cope with the complexity of life by ourselves, we can manage the complexity with God's ongoing help.

Prayer isn't just something we do at a certain time. It's meant to permeate our life, so that we pray repeatedly and often, so much so that we can say it's how we manage our lives.

I think this is what Paul meant when he told us to pray without ceasing (1 Thess. 5:17). It's not that we should spend all day in formal prayer. We should, however, live all of life aware of God's presence, interacting with Him and weaving prayer into how we live our lives. Prayer isn't just something we do at a certain time. It's meant to permeate our life, so that we pray repeatedly and often, so much so that we can say it's how we manage our lives.

Second, pray at certain times about certain things. Prayer should be both spontaneous and planned. We won't develop the habit of spontaneous prayer without also learning the discipline of regular, structured prayer. I've found it helpful to pray at certain regular times in the day.

Once every day, I spend some time in prayer. I journal about what's going on in my life and the things that are on my mind. I also go through a prayer list that I've created. I pray through various categories: my relationship with God, my family, urgent requests, my church, ministries I care about, and world issues. In the past I've used index cards in each category to keep me on track.[12] Right now I use an app on my tablet called PrayerMate,[13] which prompts me to pray about a certain number of items from the categories I've chosen. It doesn't matter when you do this, but pick a consistent time and find a structure that works for you.

Then, throughout the day, I set reminders to quickly pray. My Apple Watch tells me to breathe a few times a day. I've started using these reminders as reminders to pray. Others pray at fixed times. For example, Zack Eswine thanks God in the morning, prays for perseverance and protection from temptation at noon, for friendship, food, hospitality, and play in the early evening, and for rest at night.[14] Tim Keller prays in the morning and evening and sometimes includes a brief midday "stand-up" time of focused prayer to reconnect to his morning prayer insights.[15] Experiment with finding a planned structure for prayer that works for you.

Focus on God more than you focus on prayer. Remember, prayer is a means to an end. You're pursuing God, not the act of prayer itself.

Finally, use Scripture in your prayers. Because prayer is conversation, we need to hear God speak through His Word, and then respond through prayer. We can respond to what we read in Scripture through prayer. We can also allow Scripture to teach us how to pray by using the Psalms or by using the prayer that Jesus taught us a pattern for our prayer.[16] Tim Kerr has compiled and categorized Scripture promises and prayers in his book *Take Words With You,* so we can use them in our prayers.[17] It's an invaluable tool for learning how to use Scripture in our prayers.

I still feel like a prayer beginner, but I can't imagine not being able to pray. Prayer is one of our greatest privileges as God's children. God cares about us, and He invites us to live life in His presence. He cares about us and wants us to live in dependence on Him. Through prayer we can learn to be honest and to bring all of our messy lives into the presence and power of God, who not only cares but is willing and able to help.

Core Habit Three: Pursue Worship and Fellowship Within a Church Community

I'll be the first to admit it: sometimes church doesn't look like much. Church is a collection of people who don't have much in common and who are struggling through their lives just like us. When they gather, most of what they do looks fairly routine and maybe even a little strange. Not only that, but churches are often inconvenient, messy, and uncomfortable.

> Don't let the ordinariness of church fool you. There's a lot more going on than you think.

Add to this the times that we've been hurt and disappointed by church. It's no surprise, either, since churches are full of sinners (pastors included).

But don't let the ordinariness of church fool you. There's a lot more going on than you think. The church has always been messy and humble, and yet it's simultaneously more glorious than we can imagine. It's the bride of Christ, loved and cherished by Jesus Himself (Eph. 5:22–23). It's His body, the expression of His physical presence on earth (1 Cor. 12:12–27). It's "the household of God, which is the church of the living God, a pillar and buttress of the truth" (1 Tim 3:15). The church is a "sign, foretaste, and instrument of God's kingdom."[18] It *makes* the gospel visible.

Jesus established the church, and the Christian life in the New Testament takes place in the context of church. There's no way to live the Christian life apart from a commitment to and participation in the life of a church.

We need the church. We're meant to grow and serve within the context of a fellowship of other believers. We can't live the Christian life on our own.

Here are some steps to take to pursue fellowship within a church.

Find a good church. Don't choose a church simply because you enjoy it, or shop for a church like a consumer looking for goods and services. Find a church where the gospel is "preached, prayed, sung, celebrated, taught, applied, lived, and loved—week in, week out, day in, day out, 24/7."[19] Make sure that they take the Bible seriously and follow its commands for church: that they regularly practice baptism and communion, appoint godly leaders, and practice church discipline (correcting sin in the life of the congregation and members). Make sure that it invites you into community and mission; that it gives you opportunities to serve, pray, study, be encouraged, and encourage others in the church throughout the week. Look for a church that has a gospel culture, that incarnates "the biblical message in the relationships, vibe, feel, tone, values, priorities, aroma, honesty, freedom, gentleness, humility, cheerfulness—indeed, the total human reality of a church defined and sweetened by the gospel."[20] It doesn't have to be perfect. In fact, it won't be. But if it has those things, then you've found a good church. It doesn't matter much if it's big or small, flashy or humble, or whether it checks all of our preference boxes. Commit and stay.[21]

Show up. This doesn't sound like much, but it's important. The ministry of showing up is important for two reasons, according to Hebrews 10:

- *We need it*—"Let us hold fast the confession of our hope without wavering, for he who promised is faithful" (v. 23).
- *Others need it, too*—"And let us consider how to stir up one another to love and good works, not neglecting to meet together, as is the habit of some, but encouraging one another, and all the more as you see the Day drawing near" (vv. 24–25).

We rob ourselves and others when we don't join others for worship. If church is as important as Scripture says it is, it must be a priority in our lives.

Engage in key practices. Studies show the traits that correspond with growth: Bible engagement, obeying God and denying self, serving God and others, sharing Christ, exercising faith, seeking God, building relationships, and being unashamed and transparent. They've also shown the behaviors that lead to these traits: things like confessing sins to others, attending worship services, getting involved with ministries and projects to serve others, discipling and mentoring others, praying for church leaders, participating in Bible studies and small groups, and more.[22] Most of these traits require participation in the church. It shouldn't surprise us that these behaviors lead to growth, since they're consistent with the commands of Scripture. Build habits that help you engage in these behaviors.

One of the most important things you can do, besides participating in public worship, is to get involved in a small group or Bible study. Out of all the behaviors that are tied to the markers of spiritual growth, three showed up consistently:

- Reading the Bible
- Attending a worship service at your church
- Attending small classes or groups for adults from church, such as Sunday school, Bible study, small groups, Adult Bible Fellowships, etc.[23]

THREE CORE HABITS WE NEVER OUTGROW

We need public worship *and* smaller group interaction as we engage with church.

Participate so that your pastor and leaders are happy to see you. This sounds self-serving since I'm a pastor, but it's not about me. It's about what God says in Scripture. "Obey your leaders and submit to them, for they are keeping watch over your souls, as those who will have to give an account. Let them do this with joy and not with groaning, for that would be of no advantage to you" (Heb. 13:17). Remember that your pastors are people who need the ministry of the church too. Live in such a way that you give them grace. Contribute toward building a gospel culture within the church.

We need the ministry of the church. We need its preaching and teaching, ordinances, relationships, and even its inconveniences. It helps us get over ourselves. Even more, others in the church need us. We have a role to play within God's church. We are ministers, and we rob others of grace when we withhold the gifts God has given us. There's simply no substitute for regular, joyful, and sacrificial participation in the life of the church, even (maybe even especially) when it's costly.

> *We are ministers, and we rob others of grace when we withhold the gifts God has given us.*

ENGAGE THE CORE

I've sometimes noticed in the gym that Charlene is struggling with an exercise that I find easy. *Why is she struggling, when I'm barely breaking a sweat?* I've thought.

The answer is simple: she was doing the exercise right. Unless I'm careful, I can rush through an exercise without engaging the muscle groups they're intended to strengthen. I was going through the motions; she was engaging the core. She was working harder, and she was also seeing more benefit.

It's not enough to read or listen to the Bible, pray, and pursue worship and fellowship within a church community. If we miss the point, these practices can be dangerous, not helpful. If we read Scripture just to check off the box, pray without pursuing relationship with God, or attend a great church out of routine or obligation rather than intentional engagement, we won't grow, and we'll conclude that these practices don't work.

Of course we should still read our Bible and go to church even when we don't feel like it, but we should be aiming for genuine, heartfelt, and earnest (internal) engagement with these core habits that goes far beyond going-through-the-motions (external) engagement.

Don't just practice these habits by going through the motions. Engage your core. Seek God, not just the habits themselves.

WAX ON, WAX OFF

I've never met anyone who's encountered God's grace and who's practiced these three habits from the heart—reading or listening to the Bible, praying, and pursuing worship and fellowship within a church community—who hasn't grown. Conversely, I've never met a single person who's grown spiritually who hasn't engaged in these three core habits. These are the foundational habits that we're called to practice for the rest of our lives. We never get beyond them. They shape us and help us grow in our joyful pursuit of God and in our love for others.

When Daniel wanted to learn karate in the classic movie *The Karate Kid*, he was given an unusual task by Miyagi, his teacher. He was given a series of menial tasks: waxing cars, sanding a

THREE CORE HABITS WE NEVER OUTGROW

wooden floor, refinishing a fence, and repainting a house. Daniel grew frustrated. He didn't see a connection between these tasks and karate.

The assignments, though, trained Daniel, both in his muscles and his mind. Daniel's muscle memory allowed him to unexpectedly triumph when he competed in a tournament. He mastered the basic movements and developed discipline, and it made all the difference.

The habits of reading and listening to the Bible, praying, and pursuing worship and fellowship within a church don't seem like much. We'll be tempted to see them as menial and ordinary and to think that they're a waste of time. Develop and practice these core habits, though, and we'll soon experience more of God's grace and pleasure in our lives.

The way to grow is to master the basics—a job that takes a lifetime. We never get beyond them.

CHAPTER SUMMARY

- No matter how much we grow, we'll never grow beyond building three core gospel habits: reading or listening to the Bible, praying, and pursuing worship and fellowship within a church community.
- No spiritual habit matters more than reading or listening to the Bible. Believe that it's worth it, start small, pick a format that works for you, and good tools that will help you. Enlist support from others.
- Prayer is both easy and hard. Nobody feels like an expert at prayer. Cultivate prayer by managing your life through prayer, and by praying at set times according to a plan.

- Pursue worship and fellowship within a church community. You need the ministry of the church, even when it's challenging, and the church also needs you.
- These habits seem ordinary, but they lie at the center of Christian growth. We never get beyond them.

Questions for Personal Reflection or Group Discussion

1. Which of the core habits do you practice already?
2. Which core habits do you enjoy the most? Which do you find the most challenging?
3. How can you build the habit of reading or listening to the Bible?
4. What steps can you take to build more spontaneous and planned prayer in your life?
5. What can you do to either find a good church or to encourage somebody in the church you are in?

What Do I Do Now?

- Pick one of the three core habits listed above.
- Use the seven practices in chapter 6 to begin building that one habit into your life.
- When you have established that habit, pick another one in this chapter.
- Repeat until you're practicing all three consistently.
- Notice and celebrate the changes you see in your life as you practice these habits.

CHAPTER EIGHT

SIX PRACTICES TO PROPEL YOUR SPIRITUAL GROWTH

*How I spend this ordinary day in Christ
is how I will spend my Christian life.*
TISH HARRISON WARREN

*Find out what helps you connect with God,
and make a discipline out of it.*
PETE GREIG

It was my first time sailing. We set out on Lake Ontario on a catamaran, and I was thrilled. There's something about the wind and open water that's hard to describe, and I loved every minute.

I remember having fun. And then I remember something else: the boom swinging from one side of the boat to the other with me in the way. I went flying into the water. My host, who was probably already having second thoughts about my presence on the boat, now had to fish me out of the lake and find me dry clothes before returning me home. Sailing is okay, but it's much better if you stay in the boat.

Fast forward fifteen years. Now an adult and married, a friend offered his yacht to me for a week. At the time you could take a yacht out on the lake without a boating license.

I thought about my past boating experience and kindly declined his offer. I hadn't mastered even the most basic skills of boating, and I knew I certainly wasn't ready to captain his yacht.

Advanced challenges are good, but it's always a good idea to start by mastering the basics. As you master the basics, build supporting habits that will help you grow in every area of life.

KEEP PRACTICING THE CORE HABITS

Before moving on to supporting habits, keep practicing the core habits. Each one is simple, but each one offers a lifetime of growth. After years of reading and studying Scripture, praying, and participating in the life of the church, I feel like I'm just getting started.

These core habits are foundational for growth. It's easy to get bored with them because they seem so ordinary. They aren't flashy, and they're not quick fixes. We're often tempted to look for novelty rather than in the means God uses to grow us. The core habits, properly understood, are anything but boring. They may be mundane, ordinary, and at times lack excitement, but they are also wondrous, miraculous, and beautiful ways in which we grow into conformity with Christ and who we were meant to be. We ignore them at our peril. The moment we begin ignoring the core habits is the moment we begin to stagnate.

As we grow in the core habits, though, we can begin to add supporting habits. These are meant to supplement the core habits rather than distract from them.

The moment we begin ignoring the core habits is the moment we begin to stagnate.

Some habits are easier than others. No matter whether we're practicing the core habits or supporting habits, the funda- mentals remain the same: start small; use triggers and rewards; focus on progress, not perfection; keep going, even when you fail; and hack the habits to fit you. Employ a clean-slate policy and build consistency, especially with the core habits.

As you become more proficient with the core habits, add supporting habits. Experiment with the ones that work best for you. Remember to add one at a time to avoid getting overwhelmed.

Here's where I'd start.

PRACTICE SABBATH

Everyone I know is busy. We face a never-ending onslaught of tasks and responsibilities, and our work is never done. Now that we carry our work in our pockets and purses, it's become almost impossible to leave work at work and to get the rest we need.

As a result, we live in a perpetual state of hurry. Dr. Suzanne Koven, who practices internal medicine at Massachusetts General Hospital, writes:

> In the past few years, I've observed an epidemic of sorts: patient after patient suffering from the same condition. The symptoms of this condition include fatigue, irritability, insomnia, anxiety, headaches, heartburn, bowel disturbances, back pain, and weight gain. There are no blood tests or X-rays diagnostic

of this condition, and yet it's easy to recognize. The condition is excessive busyness.[1]

The result isn't just a frantic lifestyle; it's a busy heart. "Ultimately, every problem I see in every person I know is a problem of moving too fast for too long in too many aspects of life," observed Brady Boyd.[2]

We can counter this epidemic with one countercultural but necessary practice: Sabbath. This practice is based on two truths:

God created Sabbath. He modeled it for us. It's a routine that's been part of the creation order right from the beginning (Gen. 2:2–3). He commanded it (Ex. 20:8–11). In fact, it's the longest of the Ten Commandments. God identified it as a mark that would set His people apart from everyone else (Ex. 31:12–17).

A lot of people debate whether this command still applies to us today. While others like to debate the issue of Sabbath, I prefer to receive one. The Sabbath isn't something to debate. It's something to enjoy. Christopher Ash writes:

> I hope we can all agree that the "six day ~ one day" pattern of work and rest is hard-wired into creation and therefore into the human race. Behind the Sabbath commandment lies a creation pattern. Even if the Sabbath is no longer an old-covenant religious obligation, we are simply foolish to behave as though we no longer need a day off each week.[3]

Secondly, we need Sabbath. It's a gift that we desperately need. God gives us permission to step away from our work once a week and simply enjoy Him and all of His gifts. It's hardly a burdensome gift, but almost everyone I know looks scared when I talk about it. This usually indicates that they need this gift more than they realize.

This practice is so important that this is usually where my wife, Charlene, starts in discipling others. Before we can develop habits of growth in our life, she argues, we need to make room for them by learning how to rest.

Here are a few suggestions for building a habit of Sabbath:

- *Begin to build a pattern of regular rest in your life.* If it's too hard to jump to resting for an entire day, begin with an hour or part of your day. Disengage from all your work.
- *Let go of anything that seems like an obligation to you.* If you feel like you need to do it—answer an email, run an errand, or do a chore—then don't. No obligations while resting. Instead, pursue activities that renew you. Go for a walk. Visit with friends. Pursue a hobby. Pursue activities and people that make you feel more alive.
- *Avoid pseudo-rest.* Some activities aren't rest; they're distractions. They leave us less rested than before. I've found that most activities like social media or mindless media consumption don't leave me feeling more alive than before. Avoid them on your Sabbath.
- *As you grow in your ability to let go of work and to pursue activities that bring you rest, expand the practice.* Aim to build the practice of rest until you can do it for an entire day. Be patient, and keep going when you fail. Build your capacity for rest.

Few habits have more of a difference in my life than this one. He wants you not just to *do* but to *be*. Accept His gift as an acknowledgement of your limits and as a gift of His love. Be at rest, present, and free.

GIVE GENEROUSLY

Money flows to what we value—at least, that's what we tend to think. But Jesus flips this teaching on its head: "Where your treasure is, there your heart will be also," He says (Matt. 6:21). Our heart follows our money. When we spend money on something, it changes our emotions and affections. How we spend our money doesn't just reflect our values; it changes our values and desires.

In light of this, Jesus is clear: "Do not lay up for yourselves treasures on earth, where moth and rust destroy and where thieves break in and steal, but lay up for yourselves treasures in heaven, where neither moth nor rust destroys and where thieves do not break in and steal" (Matt. 6:19–20). Jesus directs us to invest our money toward needs and ministries that make an eternal difference.

This begins with our local church community. No ministry is more ordinary and yet more important than the local church. If you haven't yet found a good local church, go back to the third core habit and do that right away. If you have found a good local church, plug in and begin giving regularly, joyfully, and generously.

How much should you give? C. S. Lewis gives the best advice:

> I do not believe one can settle how much we ought
> to give. I am afraid the only safe rule is to give more
> than we can spare. In other words, if our expenditure
> on comforts, luxuries, amusements, etc., is up to
> the standard common among those with the same
> income as our own, we are probably giving away too
> little. If our charities do not at all pinch or hamper
> us, I should say they are too small. There ought to be
> things we should like to do and cannot do because
> our charities expenditure excludes them.[4]

In the end, our giving follows the example of Jesus. "For you know the grace of our Lord Jesus Christ, that though he was rich, yet for your sake he became poor, so that you by his poverty might become rich" (2 Cor. 8:9). Not only did Jesus give up the peace, joy, and glory of heaven, but He took on a life of poverty so that we could benefit. The gospel frees us to follow His example.

Here are some ways to develop generosity:

- *See everything as God's.* Ron Blue's first money principle in *Master Your Money* changed my view of money forever: "God owns it all."[5] When we realize it already belongs to God, it's a lot easier to give it away.

- *Get spending and debt under control.* Many of us can't give generously because we're in debt and have no margin. Tackling this problem takes courage, a plan, support, and time. There are lots of great resources out there to help you,[6] and you will feel a lot better.

- *Start small.* Assess your resources and ask: What would be a generous amount for you to give right now? Don't wait until you have the money to be generous, or else you'll never start. Start where you are. Follow the same best practices for building habits: start small; focus on progress, not perfection; and keep going even when you fail. Begin by financially supporting the ministry of your local church.

- *Set a goal.* I find a long-term vision helpful, especially when my immediate situation is challenging. I don't know if I'll ever make it, but I love the idea of a reverse tithe: keeping 10 percent of my income and giving away the rest. Set a goal, and work toward it.

I love the image used by one church near Toronto.[7] It applies to our growth in generosity as well as to all the other habits that we're learning to cultivate. We begin by giving a small amount for God's work and keeping most of our money for ourselves. As we become more generous, we keep less for ourselves and give away more for God's work:

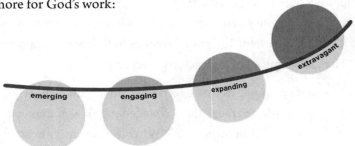

Start where you are, and grow from there.

Speaking of tithing: some people think that tithing is an Old Testament practice that no longer applies to us today. Others see it as a minimum: if the bar was set at 10 percent for people who didn't know about Jesus, shouldn't the bar be higher for us? As with the Sabbath, we can spend more time debating the issue than we do practicing the truth behind it.

While not all of us can afford to start by giving 10 percent right now, I think all of us should aim to reach the tithe and beyond, not because it's required but because we *want* to be that generous. Randy Alcorn speaks wisely to this issue:

> Tithing is clear and consistent, and it can easily be taught, including to children. It increases the believer's sense of commitment to God's work. . . . Where do you start giving? Why not start where God started his children, Israel? Tithing may begin as a duty but often it becomes becomes a delight. For faithful Israelites, unclenching their fists and opening them to God had a thousand trickle-down benefits. Is it really any different for us today?[8]

Develop the habit of generosity. Start where you are, and ask God to shape your heart as He shapes your use of money.

SERVE OTHERS

I wasn't the most coordinated child. My older brothers mocked me for my lack of sporting prowess and even the way I held a fork and knife. My oldest brother saw me carrying a computer one day in school and was shocked that somebody would trust me to carry out this task without falling.

I do okay now, but it's true: I used to be clumsy. When we don't use every part of our bodies in a coordinated way, we look funny and we just don't work right.

The same is true within the church. Paul compares us to a body in which each part plays a role and each part is important. The church needs you to play your role. Without your contribution, the church will miss out.

> *Paul compares us to a body in which each part plays a role and each part is important. The church needs you to play your role. Without your contribution, the church will miss out.*

This isn't easy. It runs against our natural selfishness. I'd rather be served than serve, even though this is contrary to the example and command of Jesus. It also runs against the way that many of our churches are structured. If the extent of our involvement in church is sitting in rows, we won't see much of a need to serve.

We're all needed. Not only do we rob the church when we don't serve, but we also disobey Scripture and rob ourselves. Studies show that serving God and others is correlated with the characteristics of a mature disciple.

The way to begin serving is just to start. While spiritual gift tests can help, I think that it's easier to just get going. Pitch in where needed. Ask others for feedback. Allow them to identify when our eyes light up and where we're most effective. Some jobs just need doing. Don't delay. Growth isn't just about maturity; it's about service.

Here are some ways to get started.

- Look for opportunities to serve, both in your church and the community. Don't wait to be asked.
- You probably don't need to take a spiritual gift test. Focus on two things: *what you do well* and *what gives you passion.*
- Don't become so focused on finding the right service opportunity. Whenever possible, just pitch in and serve where needed.
- Ask others for feedback.

SHARE THE GOSPEL

The word "evangelism" can terrify us, and for good reason. Evangelist Rico Tice admits that it is hard:

> I find evangelism hard. The problem with being an evangelist is that people assume that you find evange-lism effortless; but I don't find it easy, and never have. For me, telling people about Jesus has often been nerve wracking. But at the same time, it has been joyful.[9]

If you find sharing the gospel with others to be hard, then you're in good company. Even seasoned evangelists find it hard.

When I feel like this, I like to remind myself of Pastor Ken Smith, who wrote a letter to the writer of a hostile article against a Christian ministry. He didn't argue. He asked questions. He gently invited her to think in ways that she hadn't before. When the writer called him, he invited her over for dinner. She arrived and they began to cultivate a friendship. They listened to each other and dialogued. She didn't feel like a project; she felt like a friend. Ken didn't even invite her to church. She learned that it was safe to explore Christianity with these friends.[10]

There's so much I love about this story, and so much we can learn.

First, Ken engaged with someone who was hostile, but he wasn't antagonistic. He respected her and asked questions. It was so unexpected that the writer didn't know what to do. When we discover somebody who's hostile to Christianity, it's an opportunity *not* to be shrill, but instead to engage thoughtfully and respectfully.

Second, I love that Ken invited her to his home. It reminds me of when Steve Childers, a church planting strategist, asked, "You know what the key to evangelism in the 21st century will be, don't you?" After a long pause he gave the answer: hospitality. "Increasingly, the most strategic turf on which to engage unbelievers with the good news of Jesus may be the turf of our own homes," writes David Mathis, who heard Childers give this advice.[11] It's no surprise. Look at the ministry of Jesus, and you see a lot of food and a lot of hospitality. It's key to sharing our faith.

Finally, I notice that Ken didn't stick to the script. He didn't start by sharing the gospel. He didn't invite her to church. He didn't treat her like a project. He intentionally made space for questions about Jesus. Don't get me wrong: I'm all for sharing the great news of the gospel with people, and I'm all in for inviting people to church. But I'm against artificial pressure.

When I think of evangelism as sharing the gospel with people who don't want to hear it, I clam up. When I think of sharing the gospel as extending hospitality over good food, asking good questions, praying, and sensing what the Holy Spirit is doing, I get excited. It's something that all of us can do.

Here are some ways we can share the gospel with others:

- *Extend hospitality to people who aren't following Jesus.* Lean into these relationships, especially with people who seem like they are far from God. Make it a regular part of your life. Invite them into your home and become friends.
- *Ask good questions.* Be respectful. Listen more than you talk.
- *Regularly pray for the people who are resistant and curious.* Ask God to work in their lives.
- *Refuse to see people as projects.* Love them lavishly regardless of whether they follow Jesus or not.
- *Don't feel that you need to follow a script.* Stay sensitive to the Holy Spirit's timing.
- *Ask the Holy Spirit to give you courage to speak clearly and openly about the gospel when the time is right.*

God uses people just like you and me to spread the good news of His gospel to people who've never heard it.

LOOK AFTER YOUR BODY

The gospel is meant to change every part of our lives. Looking after our bodies is an important part of our stewardship before God for so many reasons. We're embodied beings, and we need to recover a high view of the body as an important part of what it means to be human. Because we belong to God, our bodies have become His property and residence, and we're responsible to look after them (1 Cor. 6:19–20). We can't function well in other areas of our life—including spiritually—if we don't care for our bodies.

Some people have misunderstood this command in the Bible:

"Train yourself for godliness; for while bodily training is of some value, godliness is of value in every way, as it holds promise for the present life and also for the life to come" (1 Tim. 4:7–8). They've wrongly concluded that the Bible is against paying attention to our bodies. This verse doesn't say that bodily training is unimportant. It says that bodily training is of some value. It's just not as important as godliness, which will matter for a lot longer than our physical health. That's why we've started with the core habits of Bible reading, prayer, and church community. But our bodies still matter.

It's important, then, to develop habits that help us look after our bodies. Here are a few ways to start:

- *Develop some good eating habits.* The Bible addresses this as a spiritual issue (Prov. 23:19–21). Eat slowly—you'll enjoy your food more and sense when you're full. Stop eating when you're 80 percent full. Find and enjoy foods that are both enjoyable and nutritious.
- *Move.* Take a walk or engage in an activity you enjoy. Make exercise an enjoyable and regular part of your day. Start where you are, and build from there.
- *Get enough sleep.* "Few things are as theological as sleep," writes David Murray.[12] I think he's right. Sleep reveals what we believe about God. Because God has given you important work and He wants you to steward your body well, get the sleep you need and trust God to complete what you're unable to do.

Books like *Full: Food, Jesus, and the Battle for Satisfaction* by Asheritah Ciuciu and *Reset: Living a Grace-Paced Life in a Burnout Culture* by David Murray, and coaching through Gospel for Life,[13] are helpful in learning to care for our bodies.

DEVELOP A RULE OF LIFE

Some things grow automatically, like weeds and chaos. Almost everything else grows as a result of feeding and intentionality. This applies to your growth. We're unlikely to grow without taking deliberate action.

That's where a Rule of Life comes in. A Rule of Life is a set of healthy habits that provide direction and growth in our lives. Ken Shigematsu writes, "A rule of life is simply a rhythm of practices that empowers us to live well and grow more like Jesus by helping us experience God in everything."[14] Another author defines it as "a holistic description of the Spirit-empowered rhythms and relationships that create, redeem, sustain and transform the life God invites you to humbly fulfill for Christ's glory."[15]

> *A Rule of Life is a set of rhythms and relationships designed to enable you to live with more freedom to love God and others well.*

Rule doesn't refer to a set of laws. It's from the Latin word *regula*, which means something done regularly. A Rule of Life is a set of rhythms and relationships designed to enable you to live with more freedom to love God and others well.

As you practice your habits, take note of the ones that make the biggest difference in your life. Also take note of the rhythms that work best for you. Customize the habits for your life with a special focus on the ones that you need most.

As with all the other habits, begin slowly. Your Rule of Life will likely change over time as you learn more about yourself and as your circumstances change. Experiment and be patient as you build a plan that works for your life.

Here are some tips on building your Rule of Life.

- *Start with the core habits* (reading or listening to the Bible, prayer, and pursuing worship and fellowship in a church community). Include a simple plan for integrating these habits in your life—when, where, and how you'll read or listen to Scripture, for instance.
- *Gradually add supporting habits.* What makes you most aware of God's presence and love? What other habits bring you life and joy? Keep it simple. Don't make it too complicated.
- *Think through your roles, responsibilities, and rhythms.* Be sure to include practices that help you fulfill your responsibilities in your major roles, like family and work. Begin to think through how to integrate your habits in the daily, weekly, monthly, quarterly, and annual rhythms of your life.
- *Adapt.* Some of us function best in the morning; others come awake at night. Some thrive when they work alone; others work best with others. Some of us like structure, while others prefer flexibility. Think through what works for you, and adapt your Rule so that it fits you.
- *Simplify.* When building a rule of life, many try to do too much at once. A Rule of Life isn't meant to be overwhelming. Prune yours until it's realistic. Emphasize the areas that are most strategic for you right now, and plan realistically. Consider your existing commitments, energy level, and stage of life. If you're not able to follow your Rule of Life 80 percent of the time, remove or reduce items until you can.

Shigematsu writes, "The goal of having a rule is not to achieve a 'balanced life' per se, but to live with Christ at the center of all we do."[16] It's to increase our capacity to love and serve God and others. Check out Appendix 2 for some examples.

Reminders

I've given you three core habits and six supporting habits. If you try to implement everything at once, you'll fail. Don't even start to build supporting habits until you've got the core habits in place. Keep working on those; these habits can wait until you're ready to address them.

Once you have the core habits working well, start to focus on one of these supporting habits at a time. Pick one and use the same guidelines for learning habits: start small, shape your environment, use triggers and rewards, pursue progress instead of perfection, wipe the slate clean when you fail, and investigate resistance. What you do consistently matters more than what you do really well only occasionally.

When we work these habits into our lives, they begin to work on us. They'll put us in the path of God's grace and shape our hearts. Build habits, and they'll help to build you.

CHAPTER SUMMARY

- Once the core habits are in place, it's also helpful to build supporting habits.
- Begin to grow the habit of Sabbath: spending a day a week disengaging from obligation and pursuing activities that bring you joy.
- Begin to give generously. Start where you are. See everything as God's and get your debt under control, and build so that you're joyfully giving money away beginning with your local church.

- Build the habit of serving others, both in your church and in the community. Serve where you're skilled and passionate, but also be willing to serve wherever needed.
- Build the habit of sharing the gospel. Befriend all kinds of people. Ask good questions. Be hospitable. Ask the Holy Spirit to give you opportunities to share about Jesus with courage and clarity.
- Look after your body. Eat well, move, and get the rest that you need. How you treat your body is a spiritual and practical issue.
- Create a Rule of Life. Customize these habits so they work best for you and your life.

Questions for Personal Reflection or Group Discussion
1. Which of these habits excites you the most? Why?
2. Which of these habits scares you the most? Why?
3. Which habit will you focus on right now?

What Do I Do Now?

- Continue to build the core habits. Don't focus on the supporting habits until you've built a strong foundation with the core habits from chapter 7.
- Once you're consistently practicing the core habits, pick one of the supporting habits from this chapter. Use the seven practices from chapter 6 to build this habit into your life. Start small, shape your environment, use triggers and rewards, pursue progress instead of

perfection, wipe the slate clean when you fail, and investigate resistance.

- Continue this pattern until you've implemented more of
  the habits from this chapter, one at a time.
- As you learn about what works best for you, document
  your best practices in your own Rule of Life. See Appendix 2 for sample Rules of Life and for help on writing
  your own.

CHAPTER NINE

PURSUE GROWTH TOGETHER: OUR CALL TO DISCIPLE OTHERS

If you feel quite weak and ordinary—if you feel like a mess but have the Spirit—you have the right credentials. You are one of the ordinary people God uses to help others.

EDWARD T. WELCH

He was a little quirky. His voice had only one volume: loud, which made it embarrassing for us when we tried to slip into the worship service late. "Hello, Darryl!" He'd boom as every head turned to see who'd just arrived. His wife never came to church. He wasn't cool. But few men have marked my life like him.

His name was Don Taylor. Every year he'd take me and my friends Ted and Fred into a small room in the basement of the church, and teach us the Bible. He showed us what it looked like to be a man who passionately loved God and wanted nothing more than to know and love Him more. I remember his prayers. I remember him quoting the same Bible verses. I remember him caring about us.

Every year we graduated to the next class, and, surprise, Mr. Taylor would too.

Ted, Fred, and I came to know Jesus through the ministry of Mr. Taylor and others like him. Today we're all serving in pastoral ministry. As far as I know, Mr. Taylor still continues to serve. I have a feeling I'll be surprised one day by the number of lives he's changed.

He's not alone. My childhood pastor, Denis Gibson, never pastored a large church. Like every pastor, he had his strengths and quirks. The church he did pastor was humble and full of characters that looked like they'd come out of a novel. But he preached faithfully. He showed up in a tacky uniform on Tuesday nights because that's what the children's and youth ministries required. When my father left our family, he took an individual interest in me. His ministry changed my life.

Spiritual maturity isn't about living our best lives now; it's about living ordinary lives that become extraordinary because of the way that we love God and others.

I feel like the writer of Hebrews: "And what more shall I say? For time would fail me to tell of Gideon, Barak, Samson, Jephthah, of David and Samuel and the prophets" (Heb. 11:32)—except I swap in the names of Don, Denis, Paul, Joy, Hazel, Russ, Betty, and more. All of them were ordinary. All of them shaped my life. I'm a different man because of them.

We often think that great people influence others. They do, but our definition of greatness is usually off. Great people aren't extraordinary. Great people are people like Don Taylor: ordinary, quirky, imperfect, and faithful. Spiritual maturity isn't about living our best lives now; it's about living ordinary lives that become extraordinary because of the way that we love God and others. Pursue growth with others.

HOW TO IMPACT OTHERS

When I was a seminary student, I asked a businessman to speak to our young adults group. The subject: how to impact others. I think the word *impact* was popular back then: not the first definition that shows up in the dictionary ("coming forcibly into contact with another") but the last ("have a strong effect on someone or something").[1]

The man accepted my invitation, but he told me the topic needed work. "I can't tell you how to impact someone else," he explained. "Everyone already does this. Did you want me to speak on how to impact others *positively* instead?"

I don't think he was being nitpicky. Most of us don't realize the impact we have on others even when we're not trying to have an impact. Whether we like it or not, whether we mean to or not, we affect others around us every day through our actions and behavior. Your life has a greater influence than you realize.

We tend to believe two lies. First: that nobody's watching. They are. You are shaping the people around you more than you realize. Never give into the lie that you're too invisible to shape the lives of others. You're already influencing people more than you know.

My maternal grandmother, Christina Crocker—or "Granny," as we called her—was a frail woman. She had osteoporosis. We always hugged her carefully so that we didn't unwittingly break one of her bones. Every visit to her place involved a big dish of ice cream, and occasionally burgers from the best burger joint in

Never give into the lie that you're too invisible to shape the lives of others. You're already influencing people more than you know.

town. She was one of the godliest and least assuming people I knew. And she was fun.

Granny had four children, all of whom followed Jesus. They had ten children and two stepchildren, and most of them also followed Jesus. And those twelve children and stepchildren had a total of twenty-eight children. They've started to have children too. The impact of Granny's godly life is profound, and will still influence generations to come.

Near the end of her life, Granny didn't do much more than sit on a couch and pray. She never preached a sermon, and she certainly didn't think she counted for much. But her direct descendants will likely number a thousand people within a hundred years. Her godly life, passed down, continues to cascade through generations that didn't even know her.

Never underestimate the power of a person who's quietly faithful. You can sit on a couch and serve ice cream, and still end up influencing hundreds.

Here's the other lie we tend to believe: that our lives are too ordinary to make a difference. In our information age we are immersed in extraordinary talent. We listen to gifted speakers on podcasts. We're awed by charismatic leaders and larger-than-life giants of faith. Few of them, though, walk with us through meaningful, sustainable life change. People like Don Taylor do that when they show up in a dank church basement and teach three distracted kids. The people who change us the most aren't the extraordinarily gifted, but those who have done little and mostly unnoticed things over a long period of time.[2]

I remember a pastor talking about a lunch that he and his wife shared with a couple they mentored. In the middle of the lunch, he and his wife began to fight. The other couple looked for a way to slip out. "Sit down!" the pastor said. "We want you to see how we work through a fight." They finished their fight, confessed where they had been wrong, reconciled, and prayed. Sometimes we help others more by being honest about our struggles and flaws. Our imperfections don't disqualify us from investing in others. They're exactly what God wants to use.

Your life matters. Your imperfect, routine, struggle-filled life is a gift. As you do ordinary things over a long period of time and grow in your obedience to God, your life will change the lives of others. If you're worried that you're too imperfect and broken, then understand that God will likely use your imperfections and brokenness more than your strengths. God isn't lacking in the perfection department; He doesn't need our perfection to help Him out. Instead, He uses our imperfect pursuit of His perfection as an example for others. As others watch you follow Him in your broken life, they'll learn how to follow Him in their broken lives too.

Don't wait. Don't think you have to be perfect before you start. You're already impacting others. Be intentional about it. Resolve to not just be a disciple; be a disciple-maker, starting today.

REVERSE ENGINEERING IMPACT

There's no secret to being a disciple-maker. Paul gave us clear instruction on how to do this, and it couldn't be simpler:

> You then, my child, be strengthened by the grace that is in Christ Jesus, and what you have heard from me in the presence of many witnesses entrust to faithful men, who will be able to teach others also. (2 Tim. 2:1–2)

It's true that Paul gave these instructions to Timothy, leader of a church in Ephesus. But it's clear that these aren't just instructions for church leaders. Paul invested in Timothy; then he told Timothy to invest in others; then he expected those others to invest in others too. Being a disciple-maker isn't just for church leaders. It's for all of us.

Being a disciple-maker always starts with being a disciple.

Whenever I read this, I'm struck by how simple and effective this strategy is.

First, be strengthened by the grace that's in Christ Jesus. Being a disciple-maker always starts with being a disciple. Paul reminds us that we don't get the grace we need to influence others from ourselves; it comes from Jesus and His gospel. Our first unending job is to continually find strength in Jesus, and to be clear with others that we don't find strength in ourselves. The best thing we can offer others is our own pursuit of Jesus.

Second, look for faithful, reliable people. Paul lists only two qualifications: that they are reliable, and that they will be able to pass on to others what's entrusted to them. The bar is set low. We aren't looking for charismatic leaders or unusually gifted orators. We're looking for ordinary people who show up.

Paul mentions men, but he's writing to Timothy. If Paul was writing to a woman, like Lydia or Phoebe, he might have told her to look for reliable women. Generally speaking, men are best geared to disciple men, and women are best geared to disciple women. Both men and women are needed.

As I look around, I can usually spot some extremely gifted individuals. Their gifts are far greater than mine. I sometimes worry about them. Many of them will be tempted to coast on their abilities. They may be tempted to define their leadership by what Joseph Stowell calls "outcome-driven leadership"—leadership that's driven by results, leads with the power of positional authority, and that's competitive.

I can usually also spot what Stowell calls character-driven

leaders. They're not as impressive at first. They see themselves as followers first. They measure success by character. They "know their fallenness, are unsure of their instincts, and willingly rely on the wisdom of Jesus and godly counsel," and "energetically cooperate with others for the advancement of the work of Christ."[3] Those are the people I'm looking for. Search for this kind of person around you. I bet there are more of them than you realize, even though they're often overlooked in favor of outcome-driven leaders.

What if you can't find reliable people? Pray about it. I've found that God is good at bringing the right people into our lives when it's time. Ask God to direct you to someone who is ready to grow, and who will be able to eventually help others grow too.

Still can't find reliable people? Consider patiently coming alongside men, women, and children in the church who are unreliable, unfaithful, and challenging. Invest in them, and consider how to encourage them to grow.

Then, entrust the gospel to them. Take what you've heard and pass it on to others, who will then pass it on to others. This brings it down from theory to practice. But this is exactly the point where we're most likely to get stuck.

A lot of us want to grow. If you've read this book to this point, you're at least curious if not serious about strengthening yourself in the gospel every single day and building gospel habits. You'll do this imperfectly, and things will get messy, but the Spirit will work in your life. You will grow. God will see to it.

As you grow, it's likely that you'll spot others who are reliable. I look around the little church I'm a part of and I'm amazed at the people with whom I get to share my life. It's an incredible privilege, and I can't get over it. I can think of reliable people pretty easily.

You know where I get stuck? I think I have nothing to offer them. I get tripped up with the mechanics of becoming a disciple-maker. Who am I? How can I help them when I struggle so much myself?

Who would want to be discipled by me when it's obvious that I have so much to learn? These questions are enough to stop me before I get started.

But look again at Paul's advice, and we just might get unstuck. Paul asks us to repeat what others gave to us. We don't have to invent or improve the message. We simply have to pass it on.

Paul asks Timothy to entrust the gospel to others just as Paul entrusted it to him. I don't know how exactly Paul entrusted the gospel to Timothy, but I imagine it involved long, late-night conversations, food, laughs, and maybe some tears. I know it involved relationships. Paul took a personal interest in Timothy and befriended him with a purpose. It's not so different from what Don Taylor did with me, minus the late nights.

Think about the person who's most impacted you with the gospel. Copy that. If they invested in you relationally, then invest in them relationally. If they took you out for coffee, continue taking others out for coffee. Teach them. But more importantly, share your life with them as well as the gospel. Pass on the message, and copy, as much as possible, the way that the message came to you.

Help them pass it on. Paul describes four generations of impact:

- It began with Paul;
- he passed it on to Timothy;
- Timothy passed it on to others;
- they passed it on again.

Paul wasn't satisfied with influencing another person. He wanted that person to become someone who influenced others who would then influence others.

The greatest contribution we make may be in the people we influence who then influence others. My Sunday school teacher, Don Taylor, influenced the lives of three young boys. Each of us became pastors. We're passing on what he gave to us to hundreds, even thousands, of people. Who knows how his influence will trickle down in the coming generations? The simple faithfulness of a man who showed up and served faithfully behind the scenes will continue to pay dividends for generations to come among people who won't even know his name.

We don't need to be impressive. We often won't even know what will come out of our imperfect ministries. But if we invest in others, even imperfectly, God will often multiply that investment more than we could imagine. All it takes is a commitment to find reliable people, entrust what we've received to them, challenge them to influence others, and then to stand back and watch God work.

The greatest contribution we make may be in the people we influence who then influence others.

Forget about yourself. Get over your fear that God can't use you or that you have nothing to offer. Build into others; use what you have and don't worry about what you lack. Don't focus on the impact you will have. Trust instead that God will use those whom you influence. Think in terms of generations. Nobody will know your role except for God.

To paraphrase a famous Moravian leader: entrust the gospel to others, die and be forgotten.[4] If you do that, you will be forgotten on earth and celebrated in heaven.

THE NORMAL CHRISTIAN LIFE

I don't usually elevate the New Testament church. Take a close look at the Bible and you discover churches that are full of problems just like ours. False doctrine, relational conflict, the prioritization of comfort over mission: you name the problem, and you can find it in the early church.

But there's a beauty in the New Testament church that's worth recapturing. As I read the New Testament, I see a simple truth: discipleship happens as part of the normal Christian life. We keep looking for new ways to make it happen, but when we do the normal things that Christians do, then it looks after itself.

I want to call you to do ordinary things that will make an extraordinary difference, not just in your life but in the lives of others:

Join a church. Commit to not living your life alone, but in relationship with other ordinary followers of Jesus Christ. Yes, they'll drive you crazy sometimes, but that's the point. The church is a crucial part of God's plan, and we rob both the church and ourselves when we withdraw. Commit yourself to prioritize your involvement in the life of a church that takes Jesus seriously. (See chapter 7 for more on this core habit.)

Expect God to speak to you through preaching. We often underestimate the importance of biblical preaching. It's one of God's great discipleship tools. When an ordinary preacher, even with average skills, opens God's Word, we can expect big things to happen. When a church gathers with expectation to hear and obey God's Word, that church is poised for individual and collective growth.

Practice the "one another" commands. These don't look like much. They look like lunches and coffees together. They involve grocery runs, car rides, emails and texts, and a whole lot of intentionality. They're a series of structured and unstructured interactions in which we begin to open our imperfect lives to others, pray for each other, receive encouragement from others, and try to give more than we receive.

Stay at it. It takes eighteen years for a child to reach the legal age of adulthood, but the role of parents continues even then. Invest for the long haul. We don't change quickly. Keep investing in others, allowing them to invest in you.

None of this looks impressive. It's all ordinary. But it's how we grow, and it's how we help others to grow.

There's value in curricula and programs, but they can also distract us from what matters most: living the ordinary Christian life. When we do the ordinary things that Christians are supposed to do, we'll change, and we'll help to change others.

THE MARK OF MATURITY

I used to think that the mark of maturity is personal transformation. I thought growth meant that I'd become a better person: more like Jesus, freer from sin, healthier in my body, mind, and emotions, more loving, and better able to handle suffering and death.

I don't think that anymore. Maturity isn't less than that, but it's more. Maturity is not only becoming a better and healthier person, but helping others to grow.

How do we do this? It's simple, really. Commit to growing yourself by mastering the basics that we talked about in chapter 5. Develop the core habits and supporting practices we talked about in chapters 7 and 8. And then be intentional about loving others. Invite them into the mess of your life. Allow them to see your struggles and successes. Encourage them. Live the ordinary Christian life.

In the process of growing ourselves, we'll begin to help others grow. That's the real mark of maturity.

Imitate Me

Your life matters. Your ordinary, messy, mistake-filled life with dirty dishes, unfolded laundry, and unpaid bills can make a difference not just in this generation but in generations to come.

We tend to think that God uses those who are more gifted or

godly. The reality: God uses people humble enough to say, "Imitate me, as I also imitate Christ" (1 Cor. 11:1 csb). Paul repeatedly encouraged others to follow his example:

> For though you have countless guides in Christ, you do not have many fathers. For I became your father in Christ Jesus through the gospel. I urge you, then, be imitators of me. That is why I sent you Timothy, my beloved and faithful child in the Lord, to remind you of my ways in Christ, as I teach them everywhere in every church. (1 Cor. 4:15–17)

> Brothers, join in imitating me. (Phil 3:17)

> What you have learned and received and heard and seen in me—practice these things, and the God of peace will be with you. (Phil. 4:9)

> For you yourselves know how you ought to imitate us, because we were not idle when we were with you, nor did we eat anyone's bread without paying for it, but with toil and labor we worked night and day, that we might not be a burden to any of you. It was not because we do not have that right, but to give you in ourselves an example to imitate. (2 Thess. 3:7–9)

> You, however, have followed my teaching, my conduct, my aim in life, my faith, my patience, my love, my steadfastness, my persecutions and sufferings that happened to me at Antioch, at Iconium, and at Lystra. (2 Tim. 3:10–11)

Paul repeats this so often that we can't miss his point: People learn from examples. We imitate others. We take on the qualities of those with whom we spend the most time. We need more than guides; we need people who will invite us into their lives, love us, and show us the way. It's not only what we need, it's what we can offer to others.

People can't copy your personality, and they shouldn't copy your flaws. They can, however, copy the one thing that matters most: that you run hard after God, and invite them to join you.

Ask people to follow you. That's not proud; it's biblical. Show them your faults. Invite them into your life. Talk about how you are learning to apply the gospel. Share how God is changing your desires, and share your struggles too. Reflect with them about the ways that God is growing you. Let them see the habits you've already built and the ones you're still developing. Show them

Don't be content with your own growth. Share your life so that others follow Christ because they're following you.

how to suffer, and aim to one day show them how to die. Don't be content with your own growth. Share your life so that others follow Christ because they're following you.

We don't need you to be perfect. We just need you to allow us to follow you as you follow Jesus. It's a strategy that's simple and effective. The results will ripple through generations.

Do this for a long period of time and you'll probably never be famous, but your life will matter for eternity.

CHAPTER SUMMARY

- We don't have to be great to influence others. We just have to commit to investing in others even though we're still learning and growing.

- We don't invest in others because we believe that we can't influence others. The truth is that we are already influencing others whether we think we are or not.
- We also don't invest in others because we think that we're not good enough. The truth is that God uses ordinary, imperfect people to influence others.
- To influence others, be strengthened by God's grace, look for reliable people, invest in them, and help them to pass it on. Many of us have had someone do this with us. Simply repeat the process with others.
- Live the ordinary Christian life. Plug in at a church; expect God to move through the preaching of Scripture; practice the "one another" commands of Scripture. God uses the ordinary Christian life to change us and to help us change others.
- We learn best when we copy others. The way to influence others is to invite them to follow you as you follow Jesus.

Questions for Personal Reflection or Group Discussion

1. Who are some people who have influenced your life? What can you learn from the way that they invested in you?
2. This chapter lists two lies that keep us from investing in others: thinking that we're not an influence, and thinking that we're not good enough. Which of these lies are you most tempted to believe?
3. Who are some reliable people who could use an investment of your time and encouragement, so that they can grow and influence others?

4. God uses the ordinary Christian life—involvement in a church community, Bible intake, prayer, relationships, and time—to change us. Why do you think we often underestimate this? How can you be more consistent in living this kind of life?

5. Why is it so important to learn by example? How can you invite people into your life so that they see what it looks like to follow Jesus?

 ## What Do I Do Now?

- Think about two or three people in your life who are reliable. Make a list of some ways that you can begin to build a relationship with them and invest in them.
- As you engage in the ordinary activities of the Christian life—joining a church, listening to sermons, and living in relationship with other believers—look for opportunities to invest in people who seem ready to grow.
- Pray and plan regularly for opportunities to invite people into your life so that they can learn from your example, even if you feel inadequate.

CONCLUSION

I'm a little scared. I know how many books like this I've read and never implemented. I don't want this to happen with you.

In short, here is what I want to get across, and what I hope will happen as a result of reading and applying this book.

The gospel is the good news that we're free because of what Jesus has done to rescue us. It's better news than we could possibly imagine. Because we're free, we can *live* free. Breathe in the good news of the gospel. Relax. Soak in it. Enjoy it. It truly changes everything.

Then, set your goal: not to be otherworldly, but to find your satisfaction and joy in God. Enjoy Him and all of His good gifts. Really *enjoy*. Don't trudge through life. Pursue God with everything you've got. Ask Him to change your desires so that you want what He wants, and you find your joy in Him and the life—with all its ups and downs—that He's given you.

Know your stage, and take the next step. Keep going with an eye to helping others on this journey.

Get to know God. Yes, learn about Him, but do more than that: Get to know Him. Engage your heart in worship. Grow in your obedience as you learn to love Him more.

Develop gospel habits. Focus on the big three: absorbing God's Word, praying, and engaging in worship and fellowship within a church. Start small. Use triggers and rewards. Focus on progress, not perfection. Keep going, even when you fail. Know yourself and hack the habits so that they fit you.

Stop here. No, really stop. Read the last paragraph. If you apply nothing else, work on practicing these core habits. Breathe in the gospel, practice these habits, and keep going.

Do all of this not alone, but with others. Live the ordinary Christian life: plug in at a church, submit to God's Word, and practice the "one another" commands of the Bible. Keep it simple. Keep it relational. When you can, make it fun.

As Scotty Smith says:

> Live as close to Jesus as you can. Constantly preach the gospel to yourself. Walk closely with a "gospel posse." Risk or rust for the rest of your life. Love one spouse well the rest of your life. Never be surprised to discover how broken the bride of Jesus is; how immature and selfish you can be; or how much God loves you in Jesus. Ache for heaven and serve in this moment.[1]

And repeat.

RECOMMENDED RESOURCES

STUDY BIBLES

These are Bibles that include introductions, articles, explanatory notes, diagrams, maps, and more to help you understand what you're reading.

CSB Study Bible
ESV Study Bible
NIV Zondervan Study Bible
NLT Illustrated Study Bible

READER'S BIBLES

Most Bibles are formatted with chapters and verses. Reader's Bibles remove these, which allows you to read the Bible just as you would most other books.

CSB Reader's Bible
ESV Reader's Bible

BOOKS FOR NEW BELIEVERS

These books provide a great introduction to the Christian faith for those just starting out.

Now That I'm a Christian: What It Means to Follow Jesus
    by Michael Patton
The Walk: Steps for New and Renewed Followers of Jesus
    by Stephen Smallman

INTRODUCTORY THEOLOGY BOOKS

We're all theologians. These books explain the Christian faith clearly and understandably so that we can all become good theologians.

Basic Christianity by John Stott

Christian Beliefs: Twenty Basics Every Christian Should Know by Wayne Grudem

Concise Theology by J. I. Packer

Core Christianity: Finding Yourself in God's Story by Michael Horton

Grounded in the Faith: An Essential Guide to Knowing What You Believe and Why by Kenneth Erisman

Know the Truth: A Handbook of Christian Belief by Bruce Milne

Rooted: Theology for Growing Christians by Jeff Medders

This We Believe: The Good News of Jesus Christ for the World by John K. Akers

HABITS

Some of these books explain how to build habits. Some of them explain the habits themselves. Some do both.

Habits of Grace: Enjoying Jesus through the Spiritual Disciplines by David Matthis

The Power of Habit: Why We Do What We do in Life and Business by Charles Duhigg

A Praying Life: Connecting with God in a Distracting World by Paul Miller

Read the Bible for Life: Your Guide to Understanding and Living God's Word by George Guthrie

Spiritual Disciplines for the Christian Life by Donald S. Whitney

CREATING A RULE OF LIFE

A Rule of Life is a set of rhythms and relationships designed to enable you to live with more freedom to love God and others well.

As you practice your habits, take note of the ones that make the biggest difference in your life. Also take note of the rhythms that work best for you. Customize the habits for your life with a special focus on the ones that you need most.

Here are some sample Rules of Life, as well as a short guide to writing your own.

SAMPLE RULES OF LIFE

Brad's Rule of Life: Delight in God

Brad writes, "My intent has been to shorten/simplify these few directing thoughts; but I don't want to lose the clarity of the habits for growth that fit into life."

- A consistent early morning routine of delighting in the common graces of God (include at least 20 minutes of vigorous exercise, and healthy morning eating. By this I want to delight in the grace of health).
- Prepare the kids well for their day so that they might find delight in God (includes being welcoming, allowing

for interruptions over breakfast, caring well for each one—serving them with joy—as they begin to wake up and enter the routine of their day).

- Delight in God through the gifts and personality He has given me (includes 30–60 minutes of time each morning to work on a project or problem that might be used as a means for others to delight in God—such as writing, tackling a ministry or relationship problem, making intentional efforts for the good of the family, the church, church-plant coaching and community).

- Delight in God through the roles He has placed me in (includes determining to work hard when it's work hard time, study, sermon prep, construction projects, leadership roles and community engagement within the time frame of workable hours).

- Delight to rest in God. Make the most of rest moments (includes lunch breaks, coffee stops, supper times, evenings). Cut down on the "junk rest" in my life.

- Make much of delight in God (includes speaking often and always about the lessons God is teaching us—family and church—and finding it all joy in both the good and the sucky. i.e. rehearsing the gospel to myself, being vulnerable with D-Groups, elders life together, working to further honest and loving relationship in the most important places in my life).

Karen's Rule of Life: Simplicity

My life is busy and crazy enough, so I want to more seamlessly integrate spiritual practices with what I'm already doing, and also see the things I'm already doing as the spiritual practices they can be.

- Practice focused scripture reading three times a week. If I try to do it every day, I fail.
- Attend a regular Bible study. For me, it's usually best if that is with other women.
- Read well. I depend on other Christian writers to feed my spirit and help me grow. Regular spiritual reading helps me immensely.
- Listening to worship music when I drive. I have a playlist I've developed for this purpose, and it is a reclaiming of time that I find very helpful.
- Reading poetry or brief passages of scripture with my family before meals when we are all present. Family devotions do not work in our household. Five minutes before a meal reading something beautiful does work.
- Volunteer once a week. I carve out 90 minutes a week to take my dog to a senior's home as a therapy dog team. This slowing down and offering of time and love is a spiritual discipline for me. I don't always want to do it, but I'm always glad I did.
- I speak things out loud when I'm alone. Phrases like "I trust you." Speaking truth out loud like that helps me remember who God is and who I am.

Darryl's Rule of Life: Big Picture

I want to:

- Use the gifts that God has given me (thinking strategically, learning, writing, preaching, and mentoring).
- Avoid sloth: a frantic busyness that leads me to neglect the work I should be doing, choosing instead to live within my means (financially and with my time).
- Serve and love others lavishly, outdoing them in showing honor.
- Lay down my life to serve Charlene.
- Communicate honestly and lovingly, choosing to press into hard conversations.
- Pursue depth: old books and old truths that continue to speak in new ways.
- Keep things simple, always sticking close to the core.
- Choose to do the hard, right thing, not the easy thing.
- Live out of rest.
- Be content to preach the gospel, die, and be forgotten.

Practices

- Quarterly planning (one area of focus).
- Weekly planning (three areas of focus).
- Daily planning (three things).
- Regular patterns of rest (daily breaks, weekly Sabbaths, and annual vacations).
- Morning time with God (Scripture reading, journaling, prayer).
- Morning work on writing and preaching.
- Social media and email off except for predetermined times.
- Margin between meetings.

- Where possible, 1–2 hours free in the afternoon for focused work.
- Shut off by 5:30 p.m.
- Daily reading (30 minutes a day).
- Spend 80 percent of my meeting time with the 20 percent of people I'm mentoring.

HOW TO BUILD A RULE OF LIFE

Building a Rule of Life is highly personal. It involves thinking carefully about the practices and rhythms that work best for you. Your Rule of Life will have some similarities to others, but it will also be unique to you.

Here are some steps you can take in creating the first draft of your Rule of Life.

1. **List your categories.** Your Rule of Life should cover the most important areas of your life: God, self-care, family and friends, church, work, and more. Think about the major categories of your life according to primary relationships, roles, responsibilities, and calling.
2. **Start with the basics.** We suggest beginning with the core habits: reading or listening to Scripture, praying, and pursuing worship and fellowship within a church community.
3. **Think through what works for you.** We're all different. Some of us function best in the morning; others come awake at night. Some thrive when they work alone; others work best with others. Some of us like structure, while others prefer flexibility. Ask yourself:

   - What makes you most aware of God's presence and love?

- What do you long for in your relationship with God?
- Which practices, people, and places provide nourishment in your relationship with God?
- How do you best encounter God in His Word (e.g., reading or listening, a structured plan vs. unstructured wandering, alone or with others)?
- How and when do you find it easiest to pray (e.g. alone, with others, time of day, written or spoken)?
- What day works best as your Sabbath? How can you protect this day from chores and responsibilities?
- What activities renew and refresh you?

4. **Think through rhythms.** We all have different rhythms in our life: daily, weekly, monthly, quarterly, and annual. Begin to think through your categories, and what works best for you in light of these rhythms. Which practices will you pursue daily? Which ones will you pursue weekly? Which ones will you pursue monthly, quarterly, or annually?

5. **Simplify.** When building a Rule of Life, many try to do too much at once. A Rule of Life isn't meant to be overwhelming. Prune yours until it's realistic. Emphasize the areas that are most strategic for you right now, and plan realistically. Consider your existing commitments, energy level, and stage of life. One way to simplify your Rule of Life is include both practices that stretch you and refresh you.

It's your turn. Take a stab at writing a first draft of your Rule of Life. Keep it simple, and have some fun. Open your computer or notebook and write a draft. Read it regularly, and keep tweaking it over a time so that it becomes your own user manual for growth.

A WORD TO PASTORS AND CHURCH LEADERS

I began to think about the issues in this book after talking to a pastor who had just retired. His first post-retirement project, he told me, was to try to figure out discipleship.

I knew what he was talking about. It's easy to pastor without paying much attention to whether or not people are being discipled. We hope it's happening, but we're not always sure.

Although I've written this book for individual Christians who want to grow, I want to talk about how you, as a Christian pastor or leader, can use this book within the church.

Go first. Before we can make disciples, we must be disciples. Engage in the practices we've talked about in this book. Practice the core and supporting habits. Pour your life into others. Refuse to coast. Set an example for others of what it looks like to pursue God.

Cover the basics. The ordinary ministry of the local church is essential for Christian growth and discipleship. Never underestimate the importance of clear biblical preaching, godly leadership, and small group ministries within the church. Teach the gospel and how it applies to life. Raise up godly leaders in your church who will help you shepherd the church. Create opportunities for people to practice the one-another commands of Scripture within church. Getting and keeping the basics in place is far more important than launching a discipleship program or following a curriculum.

Help people understand their Stage and how to take the next step. Use the Growth Stages diagram in chapter 4 so that people know their stage and what they need to do to progress. Speak to the stages in your preaching and teaching. Regularly think through the ways to help people take the next steps (chapter 7), both in church-wide and individual ministries. You can download a copy of the Stages diagram at https://gospelforlife.com/leaders/.

Help people build the core and supporting habits. One of the best things we can do is to help people build core habits. Teach people how to build these habits, and give them tools to help. Make Bible reading normative in your church. Challenge people to attend worship regularly and to participate in public worship and in one-another ministry like small groups. Regularly teach and foster the core habits found in chapter 7 and the supporting habits in chapter 8.

The result will be a culture of discipleship. When the pastor and leaders are growing and mentoring, the Word is being taught, people are practicing the one-another commands, habits are being formed, and people are progressing through the stages, then we can know that we've established a culture of discipleship.

It's not complicated, but it takes a lot of intentionality.

I hope this book helps you build a structure and culture of discipleship within your church. Encourage people to work through the entire book. I've designed the questions and the applications at the end for both personal use and for small group study. You can find more resources at https://gospelforlife.com/leaders/.

I'd love to hear from you. Email me at darryl@gospelforlife.com with your questions and comments.

You and your ministry are important. May God encourage and strengthen you!

ABOUT
GOSPEL FOR LIFE

Gospel for Life exists to help you apply the gospel to all of life.
We offer courses, memberships, tools, and coaching
to help you take the next step in your own growth, and to
help churches to help their people grow.

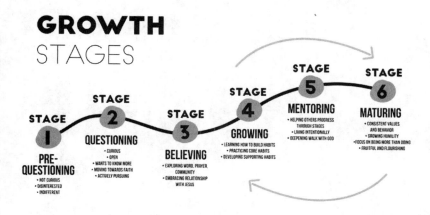

To find our more, or sign up for free updates,
visit https://gospelforlife.com.

ACKNOWLEDGMENTS

Thanks to Steve Laube, my agent, for seeing potential in my proposal, and to Ingrid Beck for taking me on and helping to shape the early drafts. Thanks also to Connor Sterchi for his editing help, and to Drew Dyck for his guidance in the final stages of publishing, and to Ashley Torres for helping me get the word out. It's been a privilege to work with the team at Moody Publishers.

I'm also grateful to Tim Challies, Trevin Wax, and Ed Stetzer for their encouragement as I began to write this book.

Thanks to my friends, who contributed to a couple of writing retreats so that I could write and edit. The Omni Penn Hotel in Pittsburgh and Warbler's Roost near South River, Ontario couldn't be more different, but both gave me just what I needed.

Thanks to my mother, who waited over forty years to collect on the dinner I promised when I published my first book. I waited too long to take you to Chez Marie, but I hope that Sassafraz was almost as good.

I used to wonder why authors don't get a theologian to review their book before it's published. It's probably because they don't know someone like Stan Fowler, one of the sharpest theological minds I know, and a good friend. I'm grateful to Ben White, Deric Bartlett, Chris Brauns, and Brian Bakke for their editing help. Karen Stiller, Brad Somers, Michael Thiessen, Barry Parker, and Jared and Michelle Polowick all helped to make this a better book.

I'm indebted to Stephanie Amores for her administrative help.

Jared Wilson is one of my favorite writers. He keeps writing great books. I'm honored that he agreed to write the foreword.

Thanks to my Nashville friends—Scotty Smith, Ray Ortlund Jr., and Scott Thomas—for continually reminding me of the gospel. Thanks especially to Scotty for his encouragement and guidance.

Thank you to Liberty Grace Church. Serving as your pastor is a privilege I don't deserve.

I could not have written this book without the support of my family. Christy, my daughter, is brave and kind. Josiah, my son, is witty and tender. Their encouragement and presence fill my life with joy.

Thanks especially to Charlene for her unwavering support and honest feedback. We spent hours discussing the ideas in this book. I'm in awe of her insight and the way she cares for people. She's the kindest, most generous, and most truthful person I know. I'm amazed that I get to be her husband. Thank you, Char, from the bottom of my heart.

Thanks also to Jimmy's Coffee, home of our weekly coffee date, the best Americano in Toronto, and now my favorite writing place.

I don't know why I've been blessed to have such amazing people around me, and such good coffee, but I'm grateful.

NOTES

CHAPTER 1: THE BEST NEWS EVER AND WHAT IT MEANS FOR YOU

Epigraph 1. Timothy Keller, "The Centrality of the Gospel," Redeemer, http://download.redeemer.com/pdf/learn/resources/Centrality_of_ the_Gospel-Keller.pdf.

Epigraph 2: Raymond C. Ortlund Jr., *The Gospel: How the Church Portrays the Beauty of Christ,* 9Marks Series: Building Healthy Churches (Wheaton, IL: Crossway, 2014), loc. 1098–1099, Kindle.

1. Alex Tizon, "My Family's Slave," *The Atlantic,* June 2017, https://www .theatlantic.com/magazine/archive/2017/06/lolas-story/524490/.

2. Curt Thompson, *The Soul of Shame: Retelling the Stories We Tell about Ourselves* (Downers Grove, IL: InterVarsity Press, 2015), loc. 98, Kindle.

3. Brené Brown, "The Power of Vulnerability," TEDxHouston, June 2010, video, 20:13, https://www.ted.com/talks/brene_brown_on_ vulnerability.

4. Wilfred M. McClay, "The Strange Persistence of Guilt," *The Hedgehog Review* 19, no. 1 (Spring 2017), http://www.iasc-culture.org/THR/ THR_article_2017_Spring_McClay.php.

5. Brian Bakke, Facebook post.

6. Martin Luther, *Letters of Spiritual Counsel,* trans. and ed. Theodore G. Tappert (Vancouver, British Columbia: Regent College, 2003), 86–87.

7. Dainius, "Student Captures What Happens When People Are Told They Are Beautiful," BoredPanda, https://www.boredpanda.com/ people-told-you-are-beautiful-video-shea-glover/.

8. J. R. R. Tolkien, *The Lord of the Rings: The Fellowship of the Ring, The Two Towers, The Return of the King* (New York: HarperCollins Publishers), Kindle Edition, 951.

9. Ann Brenoff, "Early Retirement May Be The Kiss Of Death, Study Finds," *HuffPost*, April 28, 2016, http://www.huffingtonpost.ca/entry/early-retirement-may-be-the-kiss-of-death-study-finds_us_57221aa3e4b01a5ebde49eff.

10. See Tim Keller, *The Freedom of Self-Forgetfulness: The Path to True Christian Joy* (Youngstown, PA: 10Publishing, 2012).

CHAPTER 2: WE'RE CREATED TO GROW

Epigraph: Dane C. Ortlund, *Edwards on the Christian Life: Alive to the Beauty of God* (Wheaton, IL: Crossway, 2014), 26.

1. Richard Hansen, "A Good Mystery," Preaching Today Audio issue 253.

2. John Stott, *Your Mind Matters: The Place of the Mind in the Christian Life* (Downers Grove, IL: InterVarsity Press, 2006), 30.

3. Sebastian Traeger and Greg D. Gilbert, *The Gospel at Work: How Working for King Jesus Gives Purpose and Meaning to Our Jobs* (Grand Rapids: Zondervan, 2014), from the foreword by David Platt, "The gospel brings significant meaning to the seemingly mundane and provides a supreme purpose for every employee and employer on the planet."

4. Tish Harrison Warren, *Liturgy of the Ordinary: Sacred Practices in Everyday Life* (Downers Grove, IL: InterVarsity Press, 2016).

5. Jared C. Wilson, *The Imperfect Disciple: Grace for People Who Can't Get Their Act Together* (Ada, MI: Baker Books, 2017), Kindle Edition, 9–10.

6. Dallas Willard, *Renovation of the Heart: Putting On the Character of Christ* (Colorado Springs, CO: NavPress, 2002).

7. *The Westminster Shorter Catechism: With Scripture Proofs, 3rd edition* (Oak Harbor, WA: Logos Research Systems, Inc., 1996), emphasis mine.

8. J. I. Packer, *Concise Theology: A Guide to Historic Christian Beliefs* (Wheaton, IL: Tyndale House, 1993), 169.

9. James K. A. Smith, *You Are What You Love: The Spiritual Power of Habit* (Grand Rapids: Brazos Press, 2016).

10. Jeff Vanderstelt, *Saturate: Being Disciples of Jesus in the Everyday Stuff of Life* (Wheaton, IL: Crossway, 2015), loc. 974–77, Kindle.

11. Personal email.

CHAPTER 3: RETHINKING GROWTH: PURSUING JOY AND TRANSFORMED DESIRES

Epigraph 1: Charles H. Spurgeon, *Morning and Evening: A New Edition of the Classic Devotional Based on The Holy Bible*, English Standard Version (Wheaton, IL: Crossway, 2003), loc. 5356, Kindle.

Epigraph 2: Randy Alcorn, *Happiness* (Carol Stream, IL: Tyndale, 2015), 10456–59, Kindle.

1. Cornelius Plantinga Jr., *Not the Way It's Supposed to Be: A Breviary of Sin* (Grand Rapids: Eerdmans, 1995), 14.

2. Brother Lawrence, *The Practice of the Presence of God: With Spiritual Maxims* (Grand Rapids: Revell, 1999), 116.

3. Michael E. Wittmer, *Becoming Worldly Saints: Can You Serve Jesus and Still Enjoy Your Life?* (Grand Rapids: Zondervan, 2015).

4. Westminster Assembly, *The Shorter Catechism with Scripture Proofs, 3rd edition* (Carlisle, PA: Banner of Truth, 1998).

5. This theme is found in the teachings of St. Augustine, John Newton, and especially Jonathan Edwards. More recently, John Piper and Sam Storms have written extensively on the importance of joy. See *Desiring God* by Piper and *Pleasures Evermore: The Life-Changing Power of Enjoying God* by Storms.

6. C. S. Lewis, *Letters to Malcolm: Chiefly on Prayer* (San Diego: Harvest, 1964), 92–93.

7. Randy Alcorn, *Happiness* (Carol Stream, IL: Tyndale House Publishers, 2015), 39.

8. Alcorn, *Happiness*, 44.

CHAPTER 4: KNOW WHERE YOU ARE, THEN TAKE THE NEXT STEP

Epigraph: Eugene H. Peterson, *The Jesus Way: A Conversation on the Ways That Jesus Is the Way* (Grand Rapids: Eerdmans, 2011), 12.

1. Eugene H. Peterson, *A Long Obedience in the Same Direction: Discipleship in an Instant Society* (Downers Grove, IL: InterVarsity Press, 2000).

2. Charles Simeon, *Horae Homileticae: Galatians – Ephesians*, volume 17 (London: Holdsworth and Ball, 1833), 246.

3. Adapted from *The Engel Scale*, described in a 1975 book by James Engel called *What's Gone Wrong With the Harvest*; Disciple Making Stages, a tool developed by Paul Johnson, disciple-making strategist with the Canadian National Baptist Convention; and a summary of stages on the journey of discipleship in *The Vine Project* by Colin Marshall and Tony Payne. My friends Matt Hess and Kesavan Balasingham have set up a website, https://disciplemakingstages.com that includes a self-assessment tool.

4. C.S. Lewis, "They Asked For A Paper," in *Is Theology Poetry?* (London: Geoffrey Bless, 1962), 164–65.

5. Rosaria Champagne Butterfield, *The Secret Thoughts of an Unlikely Convert: An English Professor's Journey into Christian Faith* (Pittsburgh: Crown & Covenant, 2012), 22.

6. Charles H. Spurgeon, *Spurgeon's Sermons*, electronic ed., vol. 4 (Albany, OR: Ages Software, 1998).

CHAPTER 5: MASTER THE BASICS: KNOW, WORSHIP, OBEY

1. A. W. Tozer, *The Knowledge of the Holy* (New York: HarperOne, 2009), 1.

2. J. I. Packer, *Knowing God* (Carol Stream, IL: InterVarsity Press, 1993), Kindle Edition, 17.

3. Joshua Harris, *Dug Down Deep: Unearthing What I Believe and Why It Matters* (New York: Crown Publishing Group / Mulnomah, 2011), Kindle Edition, 11.

4. Daniel Im, *No Silver Bullets: Five Small Shifts That Will Transform Your Ministry* (Nashville: B&H Books, 2017), loc. 1436–38, Kindle.

5. Bible Engagement in Canada: http://www.bibleengagementstudy.ca, and in the United States: http://news.americanbible.org/blog/entry/corporate-blog/2017-State-of-the-Bible-Report-Offers-New-Insights-into-Bible-Engagement.

6. I recommend this resource as a good place to start: *The New City Catechism: 52 Questions and Answers for Our Hearts and Minds* (Wheaton, IL: Crossway, 2017). Or see http://newcitycatechism.com.

7. Fred G. Zaspel, *Warfield on the Christian Life: Living in Light of the Gospel*, Theologians on the Christian Life Series (Wheaton, IL: Crossway, 2014), Kindle Edition, 48.

8. G. K. Beale, *We Become What We Worship: A Biblical Theology of Idolatry* (Downers Grove, IL: InterVarsity, 2008), 16.

9. Tony Sargent, *Gems from Martyn Lloyd-Jones: An Anthology of Quotations from the Doctor* (Milton Keynes, England; Colorado Springs, CO; Hyderabad, AP: Paternoster, 2007), 95.

10. Richard F. Lovelace, *Dynamics of Spiritual Life: An Evangelical Theology of Renewal* (Downers Grove, IL: IVP Academic, 1979), 210.

11. Thomas Chalmers (1780–1847), "The Expulsive Power of a New Affection," Christianity.com, March 2, 2010, http://www.christianity .com/christian-life/spiritual-growth/the-expulsive-power-of-a-new-affection-11627257.html.

12. C. John Miller, *The Heart of a Servant Leader: Letters from Jack Miller* (Phillipsburg, NJ: P&R Publishing, 2004), Kindle Edition, 19.

13. John Owen, *Overcoming Sin and Temptation: Three Classic Works by John Owen*, Edited by Kelly M. Kapic and Justin Taylor (Wheaton, IL: Crossway, 2015), Kindle Edition, 50.

14. Carl F. George lists fifty-nine one-another commands in his book *Prepare Your Church for the Future* (Ada, MI: Revell, 1991), 129–31.

CHAPTER 6: HOW HABITS HELP YOU GROW

Epigraph: Tony Dungy quoted in Charles Duhigg, *The Power of Habit: Why We Do What We do in Life and Business* (Toronto: Doubleday Canada, 2014), loc. 1046–48, Kindle.

1. Bharat Book Bureau, "The Market for Self-Improvement Products & Services," PR Newswire, January 20, 2015, https://www.prnewswire .com/news-releases/the-market-for-self-improvement-products--services-289121641.html.

2. Alan Deutschman, "Change or Die," *Fast Company*, May 1, 2005, https://www.fastcompany.com/52717/change-or-die.

3. Seth Godin, "Crash diets and good habits," *Seth's Blog*, August 21, 2012, http://sethgodin.typepad.com/seths_blog/2012/08/crash-diets-and-good-habits.html.

4. Society for Personality and Social Psychology, "How we form habits, change existing ones," ScienceDaily, August 8, 2014, https://www.sciencedaily.com/releases/2014/08/140808111931.htm.

5. Oxford Dictionaries, s.v. "habit," https://en.oxforddictionaries.com/definition/habit.

6. James K. A. Smith, *You Are What You Love: The Spiritual Power of Habit* (Ada, MI: Baker Publishing Group, 2016), loc. 329–30, Kindle.

7. From an email, November 14, 2016.

8. Andrew M. Davis, *An Infinite Journey: Growing toward Christlikeness* (Greenville, SC: Ambassador International, 2014), Kindle Location 3295.

9. David Mathis, "How Your Habits Show and Shape Your Heart," The Gospel Coalition, March 15, 2016, https://www.thegospelcoalition.org/article/how-your-habits-show-and-shape-your-heart.

10. Phillippa Lally, Cornelia H. M. van Jaarsveld, Henry W. W. Potts, Jane Wardle, "How Habits Are Formed: Modelling Habit Formation in the Real World," *European Journal of Social Psychology*, July 16, 2009, http://onlinelibrary.wiley.com/doi/10.1002/ejsp.674/abstract.

11. BJ Fogg, http://tinyhabits.com.

12. http://www.foggmethod.com. Accessed March 31, 2018.

13. Donald S. Whitney, *Spiritual Disciples for the Christian Life* (Colorado Springs, CO: NavPress, 2014), 10.

14. See Luke 11:42 for an example.

15. D. A. Carson, "Spiritual Disciplines," *Themelios* 36, no. 3 (November 2011), http://themelios.thegospelcoalition.org/article/spiritual-disciplines.

16. David Mathis, *Habits of Grace: Enjoying Jesus through the Spiritual Disciplines* (Wheaton, IL: Crossway), loc. 286, Kindle.

CHAPTER 7: THREE CORE HABITS WE NEVER OUTGROW

Epigraph: James Clear, "Vince Lombardi on the Hidden Power of Mastering the Fundamentals," https://jamesclear.com/vince-lombardi-fundamentals.

1. David Maraniss, *When Pride Still Mattered: A Life of Vince Lombardi* (New York: Simon & Schuster, 2000), 274.

2. Donald S. Whitney, *Spiritual Disciples for the Christian Life* (Colorado Springs, CO: NavPress, 2014), 22.

3. As quoted in Isabella D. Bunn, *444 Surprising Quotes About the Bible: A Treasury of Inspiring Thoughts and Classic Quotations* (Ada, MI: Bethany House Publishers, 2005), 13.

4. "The Canadian Bible Engagement Study," Canadian Bible Forum, http://www.bibleengagementstudy.ca.

5. George Guthrie, *Read the Bible for Life: Your Guide to Understanding and Living God's Word* (Nashville, TN: B&H Publishing Group, 2011), loc. 138–39, 168–71, Kindle.

6. https://thebibleproject.com.

7. Charles H. Spurgeon, *Spurgeon's Sermons*, electronic ed., vol. 17 (Albany, OR: Ages Software, 1998).

8. Jared C. Wilson, *The Imperfect Disciple: Grace for People Who Can't Get Their Act Together* (Ada, MI: Baker Publishing Group, 2017), loc. 112, Kindle.

9. Sinclair Ferguson, "What Is the Prayer of Faith?" *Ligonier Ministries* (blog), May 18, 2016, http://www.ligonier.org/blog/prayer-faith/.

10. Paul E. Miller, *A Praying Life: Connecting with God in a Distracting World* (Colorado Springs, CO: NavPress, 2017), loc. 786, 797–99, Kindle.

11. Miller, *A Praying Life*, loc. 3269–73.

12. Miller, *A Praying Life*, chapter 27.

13. https://www.prayermate.net.

14. Zack Eswine, "Taking Each Day as It Comes," *Preaching Barefoot* (blog), May 14, 2016, https://preachingbarefoot.com/2016/05/14/taking-each-day-as-it-comes/.

15. Timothy Keller, *Prayer: Experiencing Awe and Intimacy with God* (New York: Penguin Books, 2016), 246.

16. John F. Smed, *Seven Days of Prayer with Jesus: Small Group Study* (Grace Project, 2013).

17. Tim Kerr, *Take Words With You: Scripture Promises & Prayers / A Manual For Intercession* (2015). This book is also available in the Prayer-Mate app (https://www.prayermate.net).

18. Ed Stetzer and Daniel Im, *Planting Missional Churches: Your Guide to Starting Churches That Multiply* (Nashville: B&H Academic, 2016), loc. 1972, Kindle.

19. Steve Timmis, "3 Questions to Ask When Choosing a Church," The Gospel Coalition, June 24, 2014, https://www.thegospelcoalition .org/article/3-questions-to-ask-when-choosing-a-church.

20. Ray Ortlund, "How to Build a Gospel Culture in Your Church," Orlando 2015, http://docplayer.net/24794124-3-why-does-this-matter-why-must-our-churches-preach-gospel-doctrine-and-embody-gospel-culture-simultaneously-by-god-s-grace.html.

21. If you are having a hard time finding a church, consider asking friends or check these online directories for gospel churches in your area: The Gospel Coalition (http://churches.thegospelcoalition.org) and 9Marks (http://9marks.org/church-search/).

22. Daniel Im, *No Silver Bullets: Five Small Shifts that will Transform Your Ministry* (Nashville: B&H Books, 2017), Kindle Locations 1331–69.

23. Im, *No Silver Bullets*, loc. 1420–22.

CHAPTER 8: SIX PRACTICES TO PROPEL YOUR SPIRITUAL GROWTH

Epigraph 1: Tish Harrison Warren, *Liturgy of the Ordinary: Sacred Practices in Everyday Life* (Downers Grove, IL: InterVarsity Press, 2016), 26.

Epigraph 2: Andrew Wilson, "On Devotional Times: My Ten Favourite Sentences," THINK (blog), August 23, 2017, http://thinktheology .co.uk/blog/article/on_devotional_times_my_ten_favourite_ sentences#When:07:00:00Z.

1. Suzanne Koven, "Busy Is the New Sick," *In Practice* (blog), July 31, 2013, http://archive.boston.com/lifestyle/health/blog/ inpractice/2013/07/busy_is_the_new_sick.html.

2. Brady Boyd, *Addicted to Busy: Recovery for the Rushed Soul* (Colorado Springs, CO: David C Cook, 2014), 44.

3. Christopher Ash, *Zeal Without Burnout: Seven Keys to a Lifelong Ministry of Sustainable Sacrifice* (Purcellville, VA: The Good Book Company, 2016), loc. 471–72, Kindle.

4. C. S. Lewis, *Mere Christianity* (New York: HarperOne, 2015), 86.

5. Ron Blue with Michael Blue, *Master Your Money: A Step-by-Step Plan for Experiencing Financial Contentment* (Chicago: Moody Publishers, 2016), loc. 332–33, Kindle.

6. I'm grateful for Christians Against Poverty (see https://capmoney .org/). Dave Ramsey also provides some good tools (https://www .daveramsey.com).

7. Dave Adams, "Radical Giving - We're All in This Together Week 3," sermon, C4 Church, September 22, 2013, https://www.c4church .com/sermonarchive?sapurl=LytmM2E5L21lZGlhL21pLys0emt ka3dkP2JyYW5kaW5nPXRydWUmZW1iZWQ9dHJ1ZQ==.

8. Randy Alcorn, *Managing God's Money: A Biblical Guide* (Carol Stream, IL: Tyndale House Publishers, 2011), 117–18.

9. Rico Tice with Carl Laferton, *Honest Evangelism: How to Talk about Jesus Even When It's Tough* (Purcellville, VA: The Good Book Company, 2015), loc. 83–84, Kindle.

10. Rosaria Champagne Butterfield, *The Secret Thoughts of an Unlikely Convert: An English Professor's Journey into Christian Faith* (Pittsburg: Crown & Covenant Publications, 2012), loc. 290–91 and 306–11, Kindle.

11. David Mathis, "The Key to Evangelism in the 21st Century," The Gospel Coalition, October 22, 2016, https://www.thegospelcoalition.org/ article/the-key-to-evangelism-in-21st-century.

12. David Murray, *Reset: Living a Grace-Paced Life in a Burnout Culture* (Wheaton, IL: Crossway, 2017), Kindle Locations 726–27.

13. See https://gospelforlife.com/.

14. Ken Shigematsu, *God in My Everything: How an Ancient Rhythm Helps Busy People Enjoy God* (Grand Rapids: Zondervan, 2013), 18.

15. Stephen A. Macchia, *Crafting a Rule of Life: An Invitation to the Well-Ordered Way* (Downers Grover, IL: InterVarsity Press, 2012), loc. 123–24, Kindle.

16. Shigematsu, *God in My Everything*, 27.

CHAPTER 9: PURSUE GROWTH TOGETHER: OUR CALL TO DISCIPLE OTHERS

Epigraph: Edward T. Welch, *Side by Side: Walking with Others in Wisdom and Love* (Wheaton, IL: Crossway, 2015), 14.

1. Oxford Dictionaries, s.v. "impact," https://en.oxforddictionaries.com/definition/impact.

2. Zack Eswine, *The Imperfect Pastor: Discovering Joy in Our Limitations through a Daily Apprenticeship with Jesus* (Wheaton, IL: Crossway, 2015), loc. 285, Kindle.

3. Joseph M. Stowell, *Redefining Leadership: Character-Driven Habits of Effective Leaders* (Grand Rapids: Zondervan, 2017), 15–16.

4. Janet and Geoff Benge, *Count Zinzendorf: Firstfruit* (Seattle: YWAM Publishing, 2006), 102.

CONCLUSION

1. Darryl Dash, "Heavenward: An Interview with Scotty Smith," DashHouse, August 29, 2012, https://dashhouse.com/2012829 heavenward-an-interview-with-scotty-smith/.

CAN THE BIBLE HELP ME WITH MY FOOD STRUGGLES?

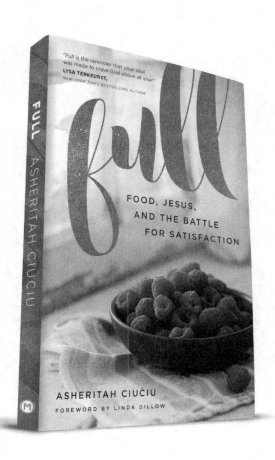

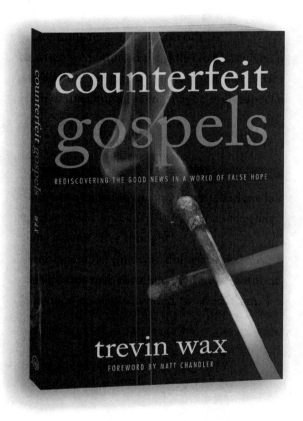